Leykam

Regional Policies in Europe
New Challenges, New Opportunities

Edited by

FRIEDRICH M. ZIMMERMANN
SUSANNE JANSCHITZ

Institute of Geography and Regional Science
Karl–Franzens–University of Graz, Austria

Graz 2000

Regional Policies in Europe
New Challenges, New Opportunities

© by Leykam Buchverlagsgesellschaft m.b.H, Graz 2000
All rights reserved, no part of this publication may be reproduced, stored in any retrieval system, or transmitted in any form or by means, electronic, mechanical, photocopying, recording, or otherwise without either the prior written permission of the publisher

Zimmermann Friedrich M. and Janschitz Susanne (editors)
Regional Policies in Europe
New Challenges, New Opportunities
Institute of Geography and Regional Science
Karl–Franzens–University of Graz
Graz, 2000
ISBN 3-7011-0029-2

Editorial organization: Institute of Geography and Regional Science
Karl–Franzens–University of Graz
Heinrichstrasse 36
Graz, Austria

Typeset and Layout: Martin Schmied

Printed by Druckerei Theiss GmbH, Wolfsberg

Contents

Editorial 7

The Eisenerz Declaration on Regional Policies in Europe 9
FRIEDRICH M. ZIMMERMANN, University of Graz,
Austria

The Third Way – A Regional Answer to Globalization? 17
WERNER A. PERGER, Die Zeit,
Germany

Guidance by Spatial Frameworks – EU Regional Policy in the Netherlands 27
WILL ZONNEVELD, Netherlands Scientific Council for Government Policy,
The Netherlands

"Regions of the Future" –
Sustainable Development through Cooperation and Competition 47
THORSTEN WIECHMAN, Institute of Ecological and Regional Development,
Germany

Nordic Periphery – Firm-oriented Incentives and Potential of Networking 63
MIKA RANTAKKO, Northern Periphery Programme Secretariat,
Finland

Technology, Innovation, Qualification: An All-inclusive Offer for Regions –
Austrian Experiences.. 81
WALTER ORTNER, Research and Training Center for Labor and Industry (FAZAT),
Austria

Demand Overflow and Sustainability – Balearic Islands 91
JOANA MARIA SEGUÍ PONS, MARIA ROSA MARTÍNEZ REYNÉS
University of Balearic Islands,
Spain

Cross-Border Cooperation: The Example of EUREGIO EGRENSIS 119
GABI TROEGER-WEIß, EUREGIO EGRENSIS,
Germany

Cross-Border Cooperation: Romania and Hungary 129
SIMONA PASCARIU, Urbanproject
Romania

Contributors.. 155

Editorial

*Our mission is to provide international knowledge and
world-class expertise for regions in Europe
through cooperation and networking for a sustainable future.*

Mission Statement of the Summer University
on "Regional Policies in Europe"

The realization of the European Union strategy paper „Agenda 2000", including its efforts to promote the Common Agricultural Policy, the Accession of Central and Eastern European Countries and especially the Structural and Regional Policy, will influence Europe as a whole and will be a further step in the changing processes of peripheral regions. Present-day phenomena like the structural change of industrial and agricultural regions, the dominance of the service sector, and the effects of modern communication technologies require new strategies. Regional initiatives launched by the European Union are reacting to the effects of globalization and are supporting regions in their change and adoption processes. Although financial support will be limited, the disadvantaged areas within the European Union will still be defined as eligible for the Union's policy funds.

The orientation towards new member countries of Central and Eastern Europe will be one of the determining factors ensuring the competitiveness of various regions in Europe on the international stage. In contrast to the European Union member countries, which hold varying positions towards the integration of Eastern European countries, the young democracies are extremely keen on becoming members of the European Union as soon as possible. The pre-accession period and later on the membership of Central and Eastern European countries will increase the need for information, resarch, education and training, evaluation and monitoring as well as for cooperation programs and joint planning far into the new millennium.

As a consequence of these current European developments, Austria has again gained the status of a mediator between Eastern and Western Europe. Professional education in the field of regional development is one of the most important factors determining the success of regions. Responding to this situation, the Institute of Geography and Regional Science at the University of Graz, Austria, in cooperation with the European Union, the Austrian government and the Federal State of Styria, established a training institution on "Regional Policies in Europe" which is intended to become a long-term offer of European relevance. "Regional Policies in Europe" focuses on the increasing demand for innovative knowledge about how to promote economic, social and environmental developments by using support strategies provided by the European Union.

The goal of this training program, which consists of the "Summer University"(a modular course system extending over three weeks) and a three-day "International Symposium", is to transfer research results into practice by using new theory – practice training tools and resources. To cope with the new requirements, the program aims at specializing on cooperation, information transfer, creativity, flexibility and permanent communication and is based upon holistic and sustainable approaches for regional development. Due to its practical orientation and its careful design the program has the capacity for fulfilling the needs of specific target groups such as regional planners and managers, environmental experts and EU regional development agents as well as young scientists and graduate students. As a medium-term perspective the installation of a post-graduate course or university course is planned.

Goals, content and organization of the Summer University and the International Symposium are based on the following principles:

- The transdisciplinary orientation helps to avoid a single disciplinary viewpoint in training and research, and it also guarantees the international competitiveness.
- The focus on practice, which is of particular concern, will be achieved by cooperating with political authorities, administration officials, experts in economy and social studies as well as by working with media and cooperating with non-profit organizations.
- The scientific basis of the Summer University is guaranteed by continuous research, whose main focus is on practical orientation, problem-centered approaches and specific research cooperations.
- These cooperations between international researchers and practitioners have already resulted in a network of information and research, the so-called EUREGNET, which is a permanent discussion group dealing with regional issues.
- The detailed structure of each Summer University is the result of an internet-based discussion and of workshops of an international steering committee
- Evaluation and monitoring of the program can be seen as further important factors which will help to maintain high-quality standards.
- In order to secure the quality of the events and to optimize cooperation between researchers and practitioners, an international research symposium will be held every year. This symposium will feature high-quality discussions of current issues of regional development by lecturers of international recognition.

This book presents the proceedings of the International Symposium 1999 and is the first book in a series which will document the results of the future symposia on "Regional Policies in Europe" and selected presentations which will be given in the course of the program over the next years.

Friedrich M. Zimmermann
Susanne Janschitz

Graz, August 2000

http://www.kfunigraz.geowww/summeruniversity
http://www.kfunigraz.geowww/europesymposium

The Eisenerz Declaration on Regional Policies in Europe

FRIEDRICH M. ZIMMERMANN

The "Eisenerz Declaration" summarizes the main results of the International Symposium "Regional Policies in Europe – New Challenges, New Opportunities" as **central messages for an innovative new period of regional development 2000 – 2006.**

In line with the objectives of the Symposium, the results will be discussed in four parts:

- Globalization trends and European answers
- Spatial, economic and social consequences of the new European Union policy period 2000 – 2006 and the Agenda 2000
- Cross-border cooperation – a new opportunity for Europe
- Lessons from abroad ... or ... examples of good practice

1. Globalization trends and European answers

1.1 Globalization and democracy

Globalization is leading to an increasing imbalance between the world of business on the one hand and democratic institutions and democratic values on the other hand. In a phase of globalization tendencies, characterized by high tech, high speed, knowledge and life in the information society as well as reform pressure on old structures, people are increasingly looking for signs of stability. LORD DAHRENDORF named this development a "new regionalism", which is developing in the form of emerging regional sentiments and regional movements as fundamental reactions against globalization. Regions and communities still seem to provide some individual protection and security to individuals, solidarity seems to bloom just in small entities.

Evidently we have to deal with this new regionalism on the one hand, but there is also a need to prepare the society for an adoption to globalization, which means to:

- Enforce deregulation to increase competitiveness
- Renew old structures and adapt to new needs
- Reduce bloated bureaucracies of administration
- Increase flexibility and efficiency
- Increase business friendliness of legal structures
- Enforce private actions by empowering the people
- Deal with life-long learning

As a consequence to increasing international influences some open questions remain:

- How can we handle and avoid poverty?
- How can we guarantee equality and equal chances?
- How can we secure new social networks?
- How can we create economic and social stability?

In taking these aspects seriously, the need arises to think about two concepts, which seem to have lost their place in our globalized society: "Redistribution" and "the Value of Values".

1.2 The European approach

The European answer to these developments is based upon a democratic, participation-oriented approach. Subsidiarity and the inclusion of people to stabilize democracy and to create new, knowledge-based and socially stable countries in Europe can and will be a competitive advantage and answer to globalization. Some questions and the "European" answers should serve to illustrate this specific approach:

There have always been structural changes! Why do we not just trust the mechanisms of market forces?

Former structural changes lasted for generations, nowadays changes take only a few years. Additionally the new communication technologies make production independent of locations, regions and nations, which leads in turn to completely new structures of markets and of competition. Processes of restructuring increase social problems and conflicts and lead to further disparities which should be avoided by means of special measures.

What is the reason for a European dimension of assistance for peripheral regions in times of internationalization and globalization?

The assistance for peripheral areas creates more stability in Europe, it develops new markets, which consequently implies an enforcing exchange of goods and the creation of a more stable economy (e.g. by improving the infrastructure). Policy measures enforce solidarity between rich regions and regions whose development is lagging behind and try to develop strong and competitive regions to avoid significant disparities with unfavorable economic and social consequences. Improving the quality of life in the periphery stops migration and avoids regional blight phenomena.

Is regional development not the task of individual countries?

Regional and structural policy at the European level is no substitution for activities on the part of individual states. *Additionality* is the catchphrase – only 0.5% of the European GDP is available for support, but should it guarantee flexible reaction to new developments. The specifics are that measures cross borders, create partnership with and within regions, and support local initiatives and local governments. Additionally they are an investment in high quality and highly specialized training in peripheral regions which ultimately leads to economic cohesion within the European Union.

The key message is that EU Regional and Structural Policy is by no means an instrument against the general economic trends, but is instead designed to support innovative and flexible economic policies.

1.3 Central and Eastern European issues

The problems of Central and Eastern European candidate countries will affect the future EU Regional Policy; The former central planning system has been followed by the implementation of basic reform steps and the development of a more or less functioning market economy. Macroeconomic transformation processes are the predominant frameworks for regional changes. There are regional impacts of the new export orientation and important economic changes like privatization, rapid growth of the service sector, influences by foreign investments, changing regional competitiveness, economic crime etc.

The impacts of these changes have resulted and still result in

- Job losses in regions with one key industry
- Job losses in specific industries, like energy, mining and arms production
- Job losses in agriculture as well as movement of jobs from the public to the private sector
- Job growth in the service sector, extremely favoring urban areas.

All this leads to a further increase of disparities and – if we transfer the political goals of the EU to the accession countries – to an extreme need for regional policy strategies, instruments, measures and support in the accession countries.

But there are lots of obstacles to transfer the EU system – underdeveloped institutional systems, weak legal regulations, a lack of instruments for territorial policies and the necessity to adapt the professional skills of territorial planners. Additionally there is still an ineffective coordination of resources and sectoral policies and a lack of financial organizational skills and control to comply with the new needs.

The next several years will be characterized by very difficult negotiations and an extremely problematic adaptation period, but there is no alternative to the EU enlargement. A non-membership scenario for the Central and Eastern European countries would mean:

- A tremendous increase of regional divergence at the wealth edge of Europe
- A decreasing attractivity for and low influence of foreign capital
- Negative impacts because of the absence of the EU – freedoms
- A serious threat of brain-drain (especially of young professionals)
- An increasing competition among European regions and enterprises.

2. Spatial, economic and social consequences of the new EU policy period 2000 – 2006 and the Agenda 2000

2.1 Some critical aspects of the past EU Regional Policy initiatives

(1) The goals of development and cohesion in the European Union are only defined by macro-economic indicators, which means that there is the postulate that social and political cohesion can only be attained through economic convergence.

(2) The programming processes of regional developments increase the need for coordination between authorities, stakeholders and the local population and improve control but reduce to a certain degree the flexibility within projects and can influence creativity and innovation.

(3) There is a strong need for training in strategic planning and long-term financing to cope with the new programming requirements and to reduce the danger of being trapped by inflexible long term planning documents.

(4) There has to be a long term financing guarantee for the national co-funding. Budget cuts in the member states endangered some innovative actions during the last programming period.

(5) There has to be a move away from the project-driven motivation of a "just return mentality", the tendency to get as much money as possible back from the EU, towards a goal-driven programming based on cooperation.

(6) Evaluation has to shift from a quantitative economic approach to an integrative and sustainable approach based (because of the length of the programming period) on improved monitoring.

(7) The increased influence of the member states in the new period 2000 – 2006 must not lead to an increased political influence and a revival of sectoral individualities.

At the Berlin summit in March 1999 overall agreement was reached on the Agenda 2000, which is the reference framework for the EU policies in the period from 2000 to 2006. Although there will be some changes in the period 2000 – 2006, there is a need for dramatic changes of regional policies, especially if we are thinking in terms of the enlargement of the EU. On July 1, 1999, the Commission decided on the financial allocation per priority Objective for each Member State, as well as for the four future Community Initiatives. In total there will be an amount of 260 billion € available (comparable figures in the previous period 203 billion €). Out of this, 136 billion € goes for Objective 1 and Objective 2 regions, decided on the basis of eligible population, regional and national prosperity, and the relative severity of the structural problems, especially the level of unemployment. This level of expenditure should enable the Union to maintain the effort towards economic and social cohesion.

2.2 Structural policy measures 2000 – 2006

Priority Objectives of the Structural Funds between 2000 and 2006 will continue to support programs in the fifteen member states but there will be greater concentration on the regions which need this assistance the most. As proposed by the Commission, the European Council decided on a reduction to three priority objectives under the Structural Funds and to reduce the percentage of the population covered by these programs from 52% to 41% of the Union's total population.

- The new Objective 1 will promote structural development and adjustment in the regions lagging in development. Eligible will be regions whose per capita GDP is less than 75% of the Community average, the most remote regions (the French overseas territories, the Azores, Madeira and the Canary Islands), and the regions currently eligible under Objective 6.

- The new Objective 2 will support economic and social adjustment in areas with structural difficulties. A maximum of 18% of the population of the Union will be covered by this objective. To ensure that all member states contribute in equal terms to a concentration of assistance, the maximum reduction in the population covered by the new Objective 2 as compared with the present coverage of Objectives 2 and 5b will not exceed 33%.

Those regions and areas which were eligible under Objectives 1, 2 and 5b (1994 – 1999) and will no longer meet the criteria for eligibility under the new Objectives 1 and 2 will receive transitional support, to consolidate the progress already achieved. This support will be decreasing and will cease at the end of 2005.

- The new Objective 3 is designed for the development of human resources (former Objectives 3 and 4). The allocations of support have been fixed according to the employment situation and the severity of problems such as social exclusion, education and training levels, and participation of women in the labor market.

2.3 The Community Initiatives 2000 – 2006

With regard to Community Initiatives, the Commission has accepted only four Community Initiatives covering the following topics:

- INTERREG – focusing on cross-border, transnational and inter-regional cooperation
- LEADER – rural development – good practice network
- URBAN – restructuring of urban problem areas
- EQUAL – new transnational cooperation to fight all types of discrimination and inequality which prevent access to employment

Additionally there will be a special initiative, called ISPA, Instruments for Structural Policies for Pre-Accession, financing the necessary adaptations and changes in Central and Eastern European candidate countries with an amount of 7 billion €. Special attention will be paid to measures, exceeding a minimum amount of 5 million €, like the familiarization of these countries with EU procedures, the development of transport links and the improvement and protection of the environment.

A further allocation of 40 billion € will be made for Structural Funds initiatives for those Central and Eastern European Countries, which will join the Union before 2006.

3. Cross-border cooperation – a new opportunity for Europe

Cross-border cooperation and partnership at the national and international level were the main challenges of the 90s. The main future challenges of areas along the external borders of the EU will be the accession of new member countries to the Union. Border areas will be much more influenced by regional and sectoral effects of the enlargement of the European Union than other areas in Western Europe. There is no doubt about the fact that there will be more advantages and chances than disadvantages and risks in the medium- and long-term perspective.

What about risks?

- There is a risk of a decreasing competitiveness of enterprises in border areas
- There is a risk for an imbalance in the labor market
- There is a risk that enterprises move to Central and Eastern European countries to use locational advantages
- There is a risk of an outward flow of purchasing power, esp. in the service sector
- There is a risk of a transfer of investments for infrastructures to candidate countries

... and what about opportunities?

- There is a chance to create common economic and social regions (tourism, culture and recreation)
- There is a chance for an improvement of locational factors through cross-border infrastructures
- There are chances for cross-border technology centers
- There is a chance for a new labor market
- There is the chance for new enterprises to use border areas as entrance doors to new markets

Major steps in the creation of cross-border cooperations can be summarized as follows:

(1) There has to be endogenous pressure and political consensus for cooperation which should lead to a cooperation contract between participating countries.

(2) The next step has to be the creation of an organizational structure, e.g. by modifying and applying different, organizational EUREGIO models to the specific needs of the cooperation regions.

(3) The conceptual work has to be based on the creation of a bilateral development concept, which needs to be detailed through regional action programs.

(4) Last but not least, operational programs will provide the framework for the realization of measures and local projects.

The management structures for the "real work" have to be based upon *project management* and permanent monitoring during the realization and implementation periods. A special focus has to be the *financial management*, especially the EU conformity of financing. *Conflict management* is one of the most important success factors in cross-border cooperations because of different languages, different legal situations, different administrative frameworks and different mentalities. This is closely connected with *information management*, especially a permanent transfer of knowledge and information, and *marketing management*, the internal and external marketing has to follow the slogan: "Do not just do good things, talk about what good you do!"

4. Lessons from abroad ... or ... examples of good practice

The final chapter summarizes the most important messages of this symposium and presents them as "Lessons from Abroad" or "Examples of Good Practice".

What are the main prerequisites for successful developments?

- The basis of all good practice examples is local, endogenous pressure and motivation. The local population, entrepreneurs and representatives need to initiate and to carry out the development processes.
- There has to be a willingness to see the value of dialogue and communication, work has to be based on partnership principles.
- Cooperation can be seen as a solution to problems of complexity and to problems of values in a development process.
- There has to be cooperation but also a healthy competition between global and local markets, states, regions and people. Get rid of the concept of "winners" and "losers". All actors must derive some benefits in order to reduce individual disadvantages, as this is the only way to achieve and foster mutual trust.

What are the key measures in successful regions?

- The creation of a learning and information network to transfer experiences into the region and to share experiences with others (no simple transfers, measures must fit with the regional potentials).
- The creation of an innovative milieu by supporting research, training and a communicative environment.
- The specialization of enterprises has to be enforced, supported by using private-public partnerships.
- Especially for peripheral areas, cooperation of small and medium scale businesses is necessary to reach critical masses.
- There has to be a participation approach including both the younger and the older generations, handicapped as well as socially disadvantaged people.
- To make these economic steps work, there is a need to develop and improve the local knowledge in the community for the region-related job market.
- Additionally there is a need for community building and the creation of a "regional environment", e.g. improvement of infrastructure, set up of a site-information system and regional marketing structures.
- The main aspect is to build on local and regional potentials and resources and set frames for private initiatives.

What are the main organizational needs for successful work?

- Focus on negotiation and mediation of different interests, using high social competence and conflict resolution strategies.

- Install regional models of organization, like regional managements, development task forces and work groups etc. to implement projects efficiently.
- Establish a regional (urban) forum, including all stakeholders and consisting of moderators, steering groups, citizens, experts, interest and business groups, administration officials, property owners and the public, as a platform for better mutual understanding and discussion to make proposals and assist in developing projects.
- Install a cooperative and professional management process in key projects.
- Guarantee that projects are implementation-oriented and constantly dynamic.
- Use a close cooperation with research institutions to improve the conceptual basis of the regional development.
- Find the unique strengths of your region and try to find your place and your niche at the European level.
- Sustainability is the key prerequisite, the realization of the development process has to be regionally and locally responsible as well as socially and environmentally conscious.

The results of this Symposium can be seen as the prerequisites for actions and measures in regional development during the following years. The discussion will continue by an internet-based discussion list and by continuing to offer this type of Symposium as a forum for the exchange of ideas and knowledge during the regional policy period 2000 – 2006.

The Third Way – A Regional Answer to Globalization?

WERNER A. PERGER

The discourse about the region as a geopolitical entity and a socio-political factor in a rapidly changing world has gained enormous importance, in particular because of this ongoing change that we have learned to call globalization. We are living in an age when almost nothing of what we have gotten used to – institutions, organizations, instruments, ways and means of living – appears to be safe from being altered, re-structured, re-engineered, downsized or dismantled. And because we are living in such an era and environment, people are looking for signs and symbols of continuity, stability and security. The local and regional environment seems to provide this kind of haven where people feel safe and wait for whatever is coming.

Indeed it is a peculiar time. We are experiencing a fantastic and unprecedented productivity and creativity, while still living in postindustrial hi-tech and hi-speed knowledge and information societies whose institutions, rules and habits are rooted in our industrial past. It is in regions like the Ruhr, the Saar Basin and Lorraine, vast parts of Spain, Pennsylvania in the United States and, last but not least, in an place like Eisenerz, where one can study this complex situation. While we realize that radical institutional and organizational change is unavoidable, our societies seem to be reluctant to embrace these necessary reforms and all too willing to resist whoever demands change. On the global level this goes for the enormous power of the interconnected financial markets and their relentless pursuit of shareholder-value. "Imagine a boat that combined the scale and mass of a supertanker with the speed and instability of a speedboat," writes the British author CHARLES LEADBEATER in his brilliant new – and quite optimistic – book about the information society in the age of globality ("On Thin Air"). With this comparison he describes the world financial system, "the force", as he puts it, "which is used to sanctify downsizing, restructuring and re-engineering". And on the national level the citizens are confronted with questions as to whether we will be able to afford yesteryear's solidarity and today's welfare in the near future – not only referring to pensions.

For many authors, politicians and activists it is the community that seems to provide some protection against the forces of darkness. RICHARD SENNETT, who is one of the most inspiring contemporary social critics, deals with this aspect in his recent book ("The Corrosion of Character"). It is the local and regional level, he argues, where solidarity seems to have a chance to survive and redevelop under the umbrella of a new civil society, which in a particular way may be better equipped to survive the structural revolutions of our time. There, where you can develop the political sensation of "We", you may get a chance "to challenge the new capitalism from within" (SENNETT). The question arises if he is right – hopefully he is.

Of course there are also great thinkers and liberal minds that remind us of the shortcomings and darker sides of regionalism, localism, parochialism and even communitarianism. They point at the negative potentials that are embedded in the new development that Lord Dahrendorf calls "new regionalism" – a geopolitical fundamentalism that nourishes the folkloristic illusion that there is a local way of containing the forces of globalization. In his important essay on the question, of whether our liberal democracies are actually at the threshold of an authoritarian age (in his words: "not an unlikely prognosis for the next century"), Lord Dahrendorf describes the emerging regional sentiments and movements in the democratic hemisphere (including the new democracies) as a fundamentalist reaction to the global developments: "The protagonists (of these movements) don't want Canada, but Quebec, not Great Britain, but Scotland, not Italy but Padania". They very often do have the backing of a majority of the local and regional population. In that sense they are democratic. But there are reasons to doubt or at least closely scrutinize their democratic quality, of which the rights of ethnic, religious and/or political minorities are an integral part. Professor Anthony Giddens mentioned the other day in a discussion that in the recent Scottish election – the first of this kind after the devolution due to the Blairite reforms – one of the competing parties in fact was running on a separatist platform – it wanted autonomy for the Scottish Highlands. So we see that the age of the dominant global players like Bill Gates, Richard Branson or George Soros also breeds a new version of Local Heroes and populist Bravehearts in all corners of our small world.

So how are we going to regain democratic territory in this permanent struggle between the political sphere of checks and balances and rules and regulations on the one side and the free markets on the other side, which have broken traditional restrictions and forcefully demand increasingly more deregulation and zero control? This is an important structural fight between the unelected elites and the elected representatives of the normal citizens, and it doesn't look like democratic politics has any home team advantage in this arena. We have reached a point at which even a man like Hans Tietmeyer, no bleeding heart liberal, shows some concern. Tietmeyer, the powerful head of the Deutsche Bundesbank until end of August 1999, having arrived at the end of his reign over the Deutschmark, said in an remarkable interview the other day that he is very concerned about the growing imbalance between the world of business and economy on the one side and politics on the other. That comes close to the question of just how democratic will our future be in a world that is exclusively dominated by shareholder value and by those whose main aim is to increase it. Is it possible to correct this imbalance, even to reverse the tide and in that sense to foster democracy?

The next chapter deals with the one current attempt to find a political answer – the **Third Way** as a European – and in that sense a regional – answer to these questions of global change. Like many new ideas in the past, it is of course highly contested in the political realm, criticized, ridiculed but also seriously debated and analyzed by the best analytical minds and it thus deserves our attention.

You should remind the outset of this journey on this particular path that this is a fairly new phenomenon on the market of ideas. It was only early 1998, when word about the "Third Way" idea started to get around, first across the Atlantic and then further on across the Channel to the more tradition-minded continent. So this was the usual west-east drift of new things. There was a gradually growing number of news-stories in magazines and quality papers which dealt with the "Third Way". At first it was not an easy task to acquire objective information as to what it was all about. You either read what was published by the authors and promoters of the new concept. Or you were entertained by those who indulged in making fun of it, denouncing the Third Way as either a new version of the first way – i.e. the classic way of capitalism. In Britain, the Tories as well as the anti-Blair left liked to call it Thatcherism with a human face. Or they criticized it as an attempt to re-popularize the old and well-trodden path of classic social democracy – the Second Way –, certainly somewhat enriched, as the critics loved to tease, with a kind of sectarian New Age language, but nevertheless pursued with the old sectarian Stalinist methods (remember: TONY BLAIR'S critics within Labour never quite made up their mind, whether to call him *Bambi* for his charms or *Stalin* for his robust methods in reforming the party). If you took this kind of public onslaught seriously, the Third Way looked like a non-starter, even with a brilliant mind like ANTHONY GIDDENS having served as its intellectual godfather – or as pathfinder, to stay in the metaphorical context.

Now, finally, since late 1998, we observe a new wave of interest in the subject – seminars, conferences, public and closed meetings are being held in many places with politicians, counselors, spin doctors, professors, economists and journalists participating and with a lot of preparatory papers delivered and papers produced after these exchanges, offering new insights, drawing political conclusions and thus preparing the ground for the next meeting and seminar. The Third Way concept is snowballing its way into an intellectual avalanche.

So here we stand marveling at this greatest success of our times in the business of idea launching. The "Third Way" is definitely not a movement of the masses; this it will never be. You may say it looks and sounds like a rather elitist movement of ruling European Social Democrats who are desperately looking for a philosophical frame for the various social-political cruelties they will have to confront their voters with anyway. So be that as it may, even critics admit that since the invention of modern campaign techniques in our so-called media age, we haven't witnessed such an astounding success as the rise of the "Third Way concept", which has a close cousin in Germany – the *Neue Mitte* or the "New Center".

Generally speaking, according to the thinkers, architects and spin doctors of the Third Way, the task is to invent a new art of governing, to develop techniques that reach beyond the old dividing lines between state-centered social democrats and trade-unions on the one hand and the neo-liberal free market orthodoxy of conservative parties and pressure groups of the employers. The government of a state reformed like this is supposed to prepare the nation for the fundamental changes that globalization will bring about. In the new era of interregional and international competition each single society has to get through this kind of fitness program. In the Third Way debate the promoters of the concept tend to underline the idea that this is the only method to stabilize the European model of the welfare state – bloated bureaucracy, increase flexibility, restructure the institution itself, reduce costs, minimize abuse, enhance efficiency. The European model may be less European after being radically overhauled – but, such is the argument, it will be much better able to survive the storms of globalization.

Today the Third Way paradigm is the dominant political topic in parties, publications, intellectual meetings almost throughout Europe. After a period of reluctance also the important social democratic Friedrich-Ebert-Foundation in Germany has picked up the issue and joined forces with New Labour in Britain. Even a well-known educational institute belonging to the realm of the still strong and influential metalworkers union of Germany, the IG Metall, did a seminar concentrating on this topic fall 1999. And in Spain in one of the many university summer courses, the Third Way was dealt with in one of the classes. There a close aide of the conservative prime minister declared in the public debate that the prime ministers party, the Partido Popular (the "People's Party") considers itself to be a Third Way party. So the Third Way is a rather broad avenue – which, incidentally, is exactly what the traditional left has always suspected.

Nevertheless the Third Way concepts, though being of great political interest across the board and beyond traditional political borders, started out as a project by the democratic left. ANTHONY GIDDENS, head of the prestigious London School of Economics and author of the widely reviewed and quoted book "The Third Way", emphasizes exactly this point: It is and remains a political concept of the left with the strategic task of reforming social democracy, of reconciling it with the traditions of liberalism and thus reestablishing the democratic left as the leading political force in democratic societies. Yet since GIDDENS' prescriptions for the social democrats call for a distinct move towards the political center – where others have already arrived and settled –, and since this movement towards the center means nothing less than moving, as far as the direction is concerned, to the right, some passionate discussion and some heavy struggle will obviously be unavoidable.

Thus we can observe basic terminological and ideological differences among Third Way proponents and social democrats in particular. The French socialists don't touch Third Way rhetoric (while the Jospin government does practice its politics, e.g. privatization, a key asset of Third Way thinking). The Jospin party plans to publish a strategic paper of its own, intending it to be a sort of counter-position to the much talked about strategic paper by TONY BLAIR and GERHARD SCHRÖDER, the so-called Blair-Schröder Paper that fueled the internal debate of the SPD in Germany.

In the meantime the message of the Third Way and its marketing success has spread to the new democracies in the east, where among the political elite there is obvious interest in the idea of being beyond the classic "left/right" division. And of course in some countries of the so-called developing world the Third Way concept attracts the interest of a new political generation which is also searching for new answers to old and new questions alike. New Third World leaders, running for office, look to the ruling Third Way parties like New Labour and the German social democrats. It reminds one of the way they or their parents' generation once upon a time looked at the Socialist International as a viable ideological option between Moscow and Wall Street. Let me give you one example: RICARDO LAGOS, the social democrat in Chile, running for president as the candidate of the coalition of Social and Christian Democrats. If elected, he would be the first socialist president of Chile since ALLENDE – but what a difference. His world and the historic world of the murdered SALVADOR ALLENDE are galaxies apart. LAGOS, before he even started to build up his campaign apparatus, went to New York to meet with business and Wall Street. To show the powerful: Don't be afraid, I like business as much as TONY BLAIR does. That is a very third-wayish approach; *Realpolitik* is the internationalized German term for it.

With all its success in the meantime, the Third Way concept has acquired a rather ambivalent reputation. As one sharp observer, RENÉ CUPERUS from a Dutch think-tank close to the PvdA (Labour-Party), put it in a recent conference paper: "For some it's just a marketing concept created by spin doctors and consultants, who try to cover up the 'betrayal' of the social-democratic project or at least try to hide what's really happening in terms of government policy behind a lot of hot air rhetoric. For others it's a term restricted to the Anglo-Saxon culture, just a charismatic symbol of the 'special relationship' between the US and the UK, between BILL CLINTON and TONY BLAIR." Both sides have their points. But while the debate goes on, one thing should not be forgotten: What has been presented so far as the Third way may not be an entirely new answer to the problems of change. But would we get any closer – let alone faster – to the solution of our problems without the debate?

The Third Way has its terminological history – actually the term itself is as old as modern politics and political movements. The radical Austromarxists in the twenties and thirties of this century claimed their position to be the Third Way between Bolshevist Communism and revisionism. The fascists in Italy and Spain and other right wing groups in Central Europe between the wars pictured themselves as the third way between capitalism and communism. And in the same era the Catholic church and the Central European Christian-Social parties (*"Christlich-Sozialen"*) spoke of a Third Way between the extremes, Bolshevism and fascism. This was later, after the war, reclaimed by the reconstructed Socialist International, a very traditional organization that was overrated by many observers. The nonaligned considered being third-wayish as well, though not using this term. And even MUHAMAR AL GADAFFI, the Libyan leader, claimed that his bizarre beliefs and politics were nothing else than a Third Way between the old ideological blocks.

Let us not forget the Swedish social democrats. They always considered their welfare state model of democratic collectivism as something very special, indeed being different from the traditional models in both Eastern and Western Europe. And finally the intellectual leaders of the Prague spring in 1968: They promoted the idea of a new political system, neither capitalist nor communist, but rather a, as OTA SIK put it so creatively, a "Third Way". More than twenty years later, at the end of the miraculous year 1989, in the former Eastern Germany the people in the opposition groups of the crumbling GDR discussed the possibility of a third option between the old SED version of totalitarian state socialism and, as they saw it, the total market ruled society of West Germany.

The Third Way we are dealing with is the latest relaunch, inspired by the so-called New Democrats of BILL CLINTON in the USA and their successful re-election campaign. It's

European premiere took place in the United Kingdom. In the beginning it was not much more than a campaign asset of the Blair-people and their New Labour strategy. The Third Way was needed as a philosophical foundation for BLAIR'S crusade against the Old Left. But it turned out to be useful beyond this internal struggle. Like in the history of some inventions in natural science, the Blair-people detected a spin off product connected with their party strategy. They found out that their prescriptions for the reform of the party might be useful for the reform of the society and the public institutions altogether. That's when they came forward with their campaign for new concepts – namely the Third Way – in a much larger dimension. And not only on the soil of the United Kingdom but rather throughout Europe. Thus the paper with SCHRÖDER. But there is also a document of mutual understanding and similarities signed by BLAIR and Spain's conservative ruler JOSÉ MARIA AZNAR. And of course there is the intimate relation with CLINTON'S fairly conservative, anti-unionist New Democrats. No wonder some people doubt that the Third Way is in fact a project of the left.

The Third Way owes its intellectual depth and political perspective mainly to the think-tanks that worked for the Blair-people. As a matter of fact quite a few of this people actually originate from these intellectual institutions. What made them so successful as seen by envious other European countries is the impression of efficiency and professionalism they managed to disseminate. Having accumulated a remarkable amount of experience in change management on the way to the electoral success, these policy planners and consultants inside and outside of 10 Downing Street hit the ground running, producing political models, pilot projects and program revisions in vast numbers. So many of these "pilot projects" are operating in fact that DAVID MILIBAND, one of BLAIRS closest advisers in one discussion recently said: "We have to watch out, that we don't have more pilots than British Airways." Trial and error is one of their principles and yes, they do consult public opinion by making intensive use of focus group techniques. But taken as a whole this approach provides for better political results than that of the German SPD. SCHRÖDER'S party came to power without a project and without any kind of blueprints for reform and policy change. This could be a recipe for political disaster.

To some extent, a good part of the British recipe for political success is a new persuasive language and a new coherent philosophy. Terms like inclusion/exclusion, rights and responsibilities, welfare to work, empowerment, active society, lifelong learning, entrepreneurial spirit, deregulation, flexibility and especially "hard work" as the non-plus-ultra for valuable members of society have become significant household words in the discourse of the Third Way architects. Obviously there are some who challenge their copyright. Indeed Liberals and Christian Democrats have argued along that rhetoric line for ages. But that it is the Left that joins the chorus – o.k., with a voice of its own, if you listen closely – that is the interesting new development that could bring about the change that we need.

What makes the Third Way so attractive for the European governments? The answer is easy – it helps to explain the social and structural changes that have to be implied by these governments, and the vast majority within the EU happen to be led by Social Democrats. For them, more than for the conservatives, it is more difficult to tell their constituents that in order to create jobs you have to be a little bit more supply side oriented in your policy – which means – more business-friendly. In such a situation it's nice to have a philosophy. It helps to make your patchwork of austerity policies look like a coherent concept for the future.

Today all 15 EU governments, regardless their political orientation, are bound by the Maastricht criteria – debt, deficit and inflation are taken more seriously than in the seventies or eighties. And there's more they have in common – the new emphasis on a modern concept of citizenship for example meaning that citizens who have rights and entitlements also do have certain obligations, that as a member of a society which is traditionally built on solidarity, the citizen has the moral duty to be an active participant in the labor market and if possible in public life too.

Although the idea that citizens have duties towards their state and society is not new, it is a rather recent topic among the reformist labor-oriented parties, especially in relation to welfare state, labor market and the paramount political question: What about equality, what about poverty, what about chances and opportunities? Or, to put it another way: What about the concept of a just society under the conditions of economic globalization? Confronted with the new menace of high-velocity financial markets that make the traditional enemy – the capitalist entrepreneur – look like a harmless character from the fairy tales of your childhood, one may ask: Where is the balance between adoption and resistance? How does the Third Way concept help to reestablish this balance? Does it have a plan for distribution and redistribution? These are questions that have yet to be answered but will have to be if the Third Way is to last for more than one or two seasons.

What we all are aware of is the difference between the British-sponsored Third Way model on the one hand and the French brand of Democratic Socialism a left-of-center reform model on the other. The French – not only the socialists – have an entirely different view of the state and its role in public life, especially in the economy. The debate about a *gouvernement politique* within the Euro-zone – as some kind of a counterbalance to the European Central Bank – is closely linked to this cultural difference. But because the French until recently never showed any ambition to present their own model of securing a just and fair society while preserving a stable system of welfare and social security, the European debate is dominated by the Anglo-Saxon/German – and also Dutch – categories.

There are of course some basics that the political classes throughout the European Union consider as being genuinely European. Their common belief is, as one can see and hear and observe in numerous seminars, conventions, documents, speeches and even policies, that state and government are more than just an administrator of what is left by the market forces, the trans-nationals, the media czars and, alas, the central banks. Market forces alone will not create full employment. Markets are good for the strong. The market is only interested in winners. So the Third Way concept is a typical European welfare state answer to global developments – everybody is entitled to get his chance to be a winner. The argument goes like this – the state is there to supply the opportunities, to – as the term goes – empower the people who are in danger of falling off the globalization high velocity train so they can, at least theoretically, catch up again and stay with it. That is the concept of inclusion, of an active society, of self-reliance and responsibility – all together new or renewed fixed points in the European welfare debate.

This concept is based on the idea of the so-called "intelligent welfare state", as FRANK VANDENBROUCK from Belgium says. It is a welfare state that should not only cover traditional social risks such as unemployment, illness and disability, old age and child benefits, but also new social risks (i.e. lack of skills, which cause long-term unemployment or low-pay employment or single parenthood). But more than that, it should also cover new social needs (above all, the need to reconcile work, family life and education and the ability to be as flexible as the new economy prefers its human capital to be).

Active government also means active labor market policies (with a delicate balance of incentives, opportunities and obligations for the people in the labor market). It involves direct interventions like subsidies for low-skilled labor, combined with decent minimum wages, hoping to stimulate the third sector in the slow continental economy.

One more thing is new in the Third Way concept regarding the responsibility-conscious reform of the welfare state: The moral aspect, the ethical background to this new approach. The welfare state that demands your decision to live up to your responsibilities may be less paternalistic than the old welfare state that looked after you regardless of the circumstances or reasons you needed it. But in a certain way it is tougher on the recipient of welfare. Behind it there is not a liberal live and let live-philosophy. Instead, the label says – no nonsense. You could say: This is social-democratic all right. But its concept of solidarity and compassion mirrors the modern ways and means of the globalization machine. It should come as no surprise that a liberal thinker like LORD DAHRENDORF criticizes the Third Way as paying too little attention to the issues of liberalism and freedom of the individual.

And there is, above all, the conceptual difference between the Anglo-Saxon capitalist model on the west side of the Channel and the Rhineland model (or social market economy) on the Continental side of the Channel. This may be in fact the most important difference, the one that the whole Third Way debate may be about: How much flexibility and adaptability and, insecurity and inequality for the working people is tolerable – or even necessary –, if your first priority is jobs, jobs, jobs. According to the Third Way understanding of responsibility, that attitude is summed up in the joyless logo: "any job is better than no job". It comes down to doing it the American way or the European way – the alternatives are not as clear-cut anymore and yet in the many debates we have always, sooner or later, reached this cultural defining line. The answer, as in many cases naturally would be: It's not either-or, it's not neither-nor. The point is the appropriate mix of both. Like in the economy, a blend of supply and demand policies seems to be the correct answer.

In conclusion: The author is well aware of the shortcomings of these concepts, the traps that are waiting once is declared reconciliation of conflicts to be the basis of the political philosophy. The class struggle is yesterday's idea, no doubt, but conflicts of interests will always exist, and on the Third Way you are bound to run into some heavy ones. Being stubbornly friendly – either to trade unions or to business, hoping this will create more jobs – can get you into trouble sooner than you expected, especially with the voters. As an old ironic wisdom has it: He who tries to avoid danger at all costs will surely perish in it. Yet it could turn out to be one of the most important impulses for our political culture in Europe, if on the Third Way we succeed in reassessing the old controversial fault lines between Left and Right or Progressive and Reactionary, Employers and Employees. As FELIPE GONZÁLEZ recently said: "We on the left have to learn that the historical enemy (the class enemy) can be right sometimes." GONZÁLEZ is right. And the same applies for the other side. Where are the business leaders who agree that the welfare state in Europe actually is one of the most important productive factors and a competitive advantage over Asia and America? That consensus would indeed be a valuable contribution to the search for a European regional answer to globalization.

To be successful the Third Way discourse and Third Way politics will need the support of the people. Otherwise the whole travel plan can be forgotten and the road maps can be put away, whoever made them, be it CLINTON, BLAIR, SCHRÖDER, KOK or PERSSON or the ex-Christian Democrat ROMANO PRODI. It is, to use a Third Way term, a matter of inclusion. Including the people in the process of change on the local, regional, national and continental level will be decisive. Our future as political citizens and cultural individuals is not a task for corporations, bankers and brokers. The future of the liberal democracy – in contrast to authoritarian post-democratic developments in some of the so-called "new democracies" but also in Asia – is our, is the citizen's business. And "we, the people", as the US Constitution so elegantly phrases it, should certainly mind our own business.

Otherwise, if change is not brought about in a democratic way, including as many citizens as possible, the whole task of structural reforms will not be a democratic enterprise. In that sense, the Third Way discourse is not in the least about the future of our liberal democracy. The spiritual architect of the whole idea and concept, ANTHONY GIDDENS, as he assesses the present crisis and the task ahead:

"Political ideas today seem to have lost their capacity to inspire and political leaders their ability to lead. Public debate is dominated by worries about declining moral standards, growing divisions between rich and poor, the stresses of the welfare state. The only groups which appear resolutely optimistic are those that place their fate in technology to resolve our problems. But technological change has mixed consequences, and in any case cannot provide a basis for an effective political programme. If political thinking is going to recapture its inspirational qualities, it has to be neither simply reactive nor confined to the everyday and the parochial. Political life is nothing without ideals, but ideals are empty if they don't relate to real possibilities."

Guidance by Spatial Frameworks – EU Regional Policy in the Netherlands

Will Zonneveld

1. Introduction

This contribution examines EU regional policy from a spatial planning perspective. At the heart of spatial planning lies the notion that spatial and spatially-relevant decisions should be made with due consideration of their spatial implications. EU structural policy can be typified as a form of spatial development policy for two reasons. First, the Structural Funds allow projects with a spatial impact to be implemented by using European subsidies. Second, the selection of regions to be eligible for European subsidies is a spatial decision in itself.

This contribution does not seek to define spatial planning. We simply suggest that planning actions for regions – which is basically what EU regional policy is doing – ought to take place within a framework which recognizes the internal structure of these regions and the position they have in a wider geographical area. Of course, the concept of planning has other connotations as well. For one, it implies that there should be a logical connection between perceptions regarding a region's present and future situation and preferred courses of action, and that these courses of action are to a certain degree consistent.

It is not beyond the scope of the Structural Funds to think along these lines. In fact, we only have to look at the regulation of the European Regional Development Fund for the 1994 – 1999 period for evidence. Article 10, for example, allows the Commission to finance studies and pilot projects on spatial development at the Community level[1]. This article was added to the ERDF regulation at a stage when the ERDF budget and other funds were expanding rapidly. Particularly the French insisted on adding Article 10 (Martin & Ten Velden 1997; Bastrup-Birk & Doucet 1997). The French felt this was necessary to provide insight into the economic and geographic relationships between subsidized less-developed regions and the more affluent ones in order to ensure that these investments were effective. Ideas and perceptions about such relationships could be referred to as frameworks. They are sometimes of a geopolitical nature, like the French "blue banana" (Lipietz).

The concept of a framework, which is central to this contribution, can also have another meaning. This paper argues that coherence in EU regional policy programs is not primarily the result of the programs or the partnerships, but – at least in the Nether-

---

[1] In the new ERDF regulation this article 10 is replaced by another article (3). The activities mentioned here which are eligible for funding also relate to spatial development. The main difference is formed by the fact that the position of the Commission with regard to the steering of programmes is played down to the observer status when compared with the "old" Article 10.

lands – the application of existing strategic plans. Therefore these plans act as frameworks for decision-making.

The first section looks at the politics of how regions are selected for funding under the Structural Funds[2]. We shall argue that the designation of Objective 1, 2 and 5b regions (in the future: Objective 1 and 2 regions) is done in a way that bears no resemblance to reasonable spatial policy. In the second section we pose the question of whether synergy exists between EU regional policy and Dutch spatial economic policy. We conclude that EU regional policy closely resembles Dutch regional policy two decades ago. The third section examines a specific EU regional policy program in detail, namely the program for Flevoland, the only Objective 1 region in the Netherlands. This will demonstrate the importance of existing policy frameworks for the way this program is treated. There is evidence that the same applies to other objective regions in the Netherlands. The final section provides some concluding remarks.

The analysis presented here concerns the background to the present state of the Structural Funds. In the 2000 – 2006 period, new regulations will come into force. Mechanisms regarding the selection of objective regions have been slightly modified. The number of objectives has also been cut back and more emphasis is now being placed on the principles of the 1988 Structural Funds revision. Still, we must bear in mind that no complete overhaul of the Structural Funds has occurred, and, by and large, the argumentation presented here will be valid for the upcoming program period.

2. Conducting spatial policy by designating regions

2.1 Objectives of the 1988 revision

In order to gain an adequate understanding of the current workings of the Structural Funds, one should examine the revision of 1988. These were the most far-reaching changes made to date, including the decisions taken in 1999 in accordance with Agenda 2000. In the goals section of the 1988 revision, one can read about the main problems which had surfaced since 1975. First, this period saw the splintering of subsidies into a multitude of projects and areas. Second, it became increasingly clear that a lack of cohesion existed between the workings of the Structural Funds, which were controlled by three separate directorate-generals in Brussels. Third, there was a lack of clarity about the nature of European subsidies, as these were not supposed to serve as a substitute for budgetary expenditures from the member states' governments.

The revision of 1988 corresponded to the entrance of Spain and Portugal into the European Union in 1986 (BACHTLER & MICHIE 1993). Using the average GDP of the member states as the mean, the inclusion of these less-affluent countries (at that time, some called Portugal "the sickly one in Europe") caused an abrupt increase in the regional disparities within the EU. The Single European Act of 1986, which came

---

[2] This paper is based on a research project commissioned by the Netherlands Scientific Council for Governmental Policy (ZONNEVELD & FALUDI 1997).

into force in mid-1987, also stated that economic and social cohesion in the EU was an essential component in the creation of the Single Market. This heavy political endorsement of the cohesion principle went hand in hand with a rapidly swelling Structural Funds budget from 6.3 billion € in 1987, 9.1 billion € in 1989, to 14.1 billion € in 1993.

The revision of the Structural Funds was linked to the introduction of four key principles (EUROPEAN COMMISSION 1996):

- *concentration* of measures into a package of primary objectives (five in total; a sixth was added through the negotiations for the 1995 enlargement; WILLIAMS 1996: 121). The aim was to prompt both a financial and a geographic concentration of the eligible funds

- *programming* of activity into long-range development schemes to be worked out in a number of phases; these were to specify the individual actions to be carried out by the government or business community

- *partnership* between the Commission and all the authorized bodies identified by the member states at the national, regional, or local level in all programming phases. This implies close cooperation from the preparation of development programs up to and including their execution

- *additionality*; meaning that EU subsidies cannot be accompanied by cutbacks in national efforts: both must supplement each other. Except in special cases, all member states must maintain the level of expenditure for each objective at at least the level of the preceding period.

One of the main bottlenecks of the previous period did not disappear with the 1988 revision: the parallel existence of three funds, each managed by its own directorate-general at the European Commission level. Although integration received marginal attention during the review process, this was, for all practical purposes, a non-issue. As integration would bring about considerable power shifts within the European Commission, no iota of support could be found among bureaucrats (directorate-generals) or politicians (commissioners). The 1988 revision of the Structural Funds and the later, more modest amendments in 1993 mainly impacted the application of the funds. A framework regulation was placed "above" the regulations that governed the separate Structural Funds[3]. Each of the separate fund regulations describes which measures and activities would be eligible for funding from that source.

---

[3] EEC Regulation no.2052/88 concerning the tasks of the Funds with structural reach, their effectiveness as well as the coordination of their welfare provision individually and in conjunction with that of the European Investment Bank and other financial instruments (OFFICIAL JOURNAL OF THE EUROPEAN COMMUNITIES, No. L185, July 15, 1988).

> The principle of concentrating the Structural Funds has been fleshed out into the following objectives. According to the text of the somewhat-revised framework regulation of July 1993[4], these are:
>
> 1. promoting the development and Structural adjustment of regions whose development is lagging behind
>
> 2. converting the regions, frontier regions or parts of regions (including employment areas and urban communities) seriously affected by industrial decline
>
> 3. combating long-term unemployment and facilitating the integration into working life of young people and of persons exposed to exclusion from the labor market
>
> 4. facilitating the adaptation of workers of either sex to industrial changes and to changes in production systems
>
> 5. promoting rural development by:
>   a) speeding up the adjustment of agricultural structures in the framework of the reform of the common agricultural policy
>   b) facilitating the development and structural adjustment of rural areas
>
> Added later is Objective 6 (basically, following WILLIAMS 1996, an Arctic version of Objective 1): economic adjustment of regions with outstandingly low population density.

By far the largest part of the Structural Funds is channeled towards meeting the objectives listed in the box above. This takes place by means of programs initiated by the member states. This comprises 90% of the total Structural Funds budget for the current period (1994 – 1999). The remaining 10% is reserved for activities for which the European Commission has discretion.

2.2 Spatial implication of the Structural Funds

From the perspective of spatial planning, the Structural Funds are interesting for two reasons. First, they allow projects with a spatial impact to be carried out using European subsidies. However, this paper is not so much concerned with the immediately observable spatial effects of European programs. Instead, it concentrates on the systems that govern decision-making on projects that have (or could have) clear spatial impacts. This is reflected in the Dutch programs and the second spatial impact of European structural policy: the selection of regions to receive funding.

The six objectives of the Structural Funds can be divided into two main groups. First, those which are horizontal in nature because they apply to the entire territory of the EU (Objectives 3, 4 and 5a). The others relate to specific areas and are thus referred to as regional objectives. The regions concerned (Objectives 1 and 6) and zones (Objectives 2 and 5b) are identified as Objective 1, 2, 5b and 6 regions.

---

[4] Council Regulation (EEC) no.2081/93 of 20 July 1993 amending Regulation (EEC) no.2052/88 on the tasks of the Structural Funds and their effectiveness, and on coordination of their activities amongst themselves as well as with the operations of the European Investment Bank and other existing financial instruments (OFFICIAL JOURNAL OF THE EUROPEAN COMMUNITIES, No.L193, July 31, 1993).

Of the three horizontal objectives, the employment Objectives (3 and 4) have a direct but modest spatial impact. They mainly emphasize education, training, and other measures to involve the unemployed in the labor process or to combat impending unemployment. Subsidies granted in the context of this objective come exclusively from the European Social Funds. Objective 5a, fed from EAGGF and FIFG sources, can have a spatial impact, especially if the measures relate to the agricultural structure[5]. As stated above, the other objectives relate to the designation of areas.

The process of designating areas for Structural Funds money is a classic example one of the many convoluted decision-making spectacles that abound within the European Union. The budgets for a programming period are determined by the Council of the European Communities. Since this entails astronomical budgets, the Councils involved in the process have considerable political clout. Not surprisingly, the decision-making round for the 1994 – 1999 period was grueling.

Not only the budgets themselves, but also the mechanisms for their allocation is extremely sensitive political terrain. This was even apparent in the decision-making procedure to be followed. The relevant article in the EC Treaty (art. 130d) stipulates that the Council "acting unanimously ... shall define the tasks, priority objectives and the organization of the Structural Funds ..."[6]. In other words, unanimity is required for both establishing and amending a framework regulation. Furthermore, this article falls under the co-called assent procedure – a procedure "not used for 'normal' legislation but ... reserved for special types of decision" (NUGENT 1999: 374). As the name suggests, one can only vote for it or against it. CORBETT et al (1995) conclude that a "take it or leave it" stance is common when it concerns the approval of international treaties by national parliaments. It is also quite common with regard to constitutional decision-making. "However, its application to measures which are typically legislative in character, such as the operational rules for the Structural Funds, is curious" (ibid. pp. 212). The assent procedure has created a situation where the European Parliament is unable to "tinker" with the criteria that will ultimately determine the areas to qualify for Structural fund subsidies.

The framework regulation provides an array of hard, but mostly soft – and thus politically negotiable – criteria for the designation of target areas. Of all the target areas, the criteria for Objective 1 regions are the most rigid. It is mainly thanks to the European Parliament that this criterion was included in the framework regulation in the way it was. The European Parliament wanted to maintain an "objective" standard to determine those kinds of areas for which the most subsidies would be made available (MINEKUS 1994). Seventy percent of the entire Structural Funds budget flows into these areas. It is therefore the Council which designates Objective 1 regions, and the Commission which selects the rest "in consultation with the member states and taking into account the relevant criteria set for this" (BRUINSMA 1996: 14). The criterion used for selection and delineation is:

---

[5] Regulations can be found under the Objective 5a policy which relate to the fishery structure. Since the revision, the European structural policy has been split off from the EOGFL-O and subsumed under a new "instrument": the Funding Instrument for the Orientation of Fisheries (FIFG).

[6] In the new EC Treaty this is article 161.

The regions covered by Objective 1 shall be regions at NUTS level II whose per capita GDP, on the basis of figures for the last three years, is less than 75% of the Community average.

The framework regulation for the upcoming period stipulates that the per capita GDP should be measured in parities of purchasing power. The intent and result of this will be that regions in more affluent EU member states like the Netherlands will no longer be eligible for Objective 1 subsidies. It is also striking (and this is still the case in the new regulation), that the location and size of the area are expressed as statistical quantities. The selection is made on the basis of a classification which has not been specifically developed for policy purposes, let alone spatial policy purposes. NUTS is an acronym for *Nomenclature des Unités Territoriales Statistiques*, and as the name suggests, is primarily concerned with compiling statistical data into comparable units (SCHOBBEN 1995). The NUTS classification is identical to the regional classification maintained by the member states.

The NUTS I level refers to units such as the four Dutch regions, British standard regions, regions or *Länder* in Germany and Austria, and the entire countries of Denmark, Ireland and Luxembourg. The NUTS II level produces a fairly heterogeneous picture, although the link to established governmental authorities is more apparent. This level includes entities such as the provinces of the Netherlands and Belgium, the *Regierungsbezirke* in Germany and groups of counties in the UK. The three countries whose entire territory falls into a NUTS I area are not divided up as much. This may make sense for Luxembourg, but it is much less appropriate for Denmark and Ireland. The NUTS III level shows a mosaic of various kinds of small regions which in most (but not all) cases correspond to administrative boundaries. The forty Dutch COROP areas, for example, show up at this level[7].

In short, each NUTS level contains territorial units which can differ drastically from country to country not only in terms of scale, but also in terms of the public authorities residing at that level. Sometimes a region specified at a given NUTS level will have absolutely no jurisdictional authority whatsoever. Public authorities in the UK are only encountered at the NUTS III level, which is a good indication of the extremely high degree of administrative centralization in that country. In other words, the NUTS classification usually produces a division into regions which, when compared to other member states, point to completely different spatial entities. Meanwhile the NUTS classification continues to be used for policy purposes with a powerful spatial component.

Be this as it may, if a region satisfies the criteria for Objective 1 status, then the designation of an area is almost assured, provided that the area is officially put forward by the member state. The provisions regarding the other objective regions allow much more room for interpretation and negotiation.

---

[7] COROP-regions are purely statistical regions (the acronym is derived from the name of the Committee proposing these regions).

Although Objective 2 regions also have hard basic criteria, they also include an entire spectrum of flexible criteria that the member states can employ when putting forward areas to the Commission. The basic criteria are the following:

- the average rate of unemployment recorded over the last three years must have been above the Community average
- the percentage share of industrial employment in total employment must have equaled or exceeded the Community average in any reference year from 1975 onwards
- there must have been an observable drop in industrial employment compared with the reference year chosen in accordance with (b).

The flexibility can mainly be found in a number of criteria for "zones" which do not initially satisfy the hard basic criteria such as proximity to Objective 1 regions, although the framework regulation also stipulates that the Commission and the member states shall seek "to ensure that assistance is genuinely concentrated on the areas most seriously affected."

The spatial pattern of Objective 2 regions in the European Union shows a very fragmented picture. Although some leeway exists in the NUTS classification, as stated above, Objective 1 regions have a minimum size requirement of NUTS II. This is not the case for Objective 2 regions. At the level of NUTS III regions (in theory the level of scale for Objective 2 regions), member states are allowed to shift borders around in such a manner that the remaining "zones" will meet some of the criteria in the framework regulation. The procedure for designating Objective 2 regions is extremely complex, and the number of areas which were finally selected (5 in the Netherlands) is phenomenal. Whereas the names of all the Objective 1 regions can fit on half a sheet of paper, the list of Objective 2 regions is 52 pages long according to WILLIAMS (1996). And yet the total budget for the 1994 – 1999 period is less than a sixth of that for Objective 1 regions! It is therefore not surprising that the philosophy of concentration has become fairly watered-down as far as Objective 2 regions are concerned. The programs for the different areas also vary widely in size. The smallest program in the first[8] programming period for Objective 2 regions (1994 – 1996) – Aubange, Belgium – is almost 400 times smaller than Catalonia, the largest program (1.3 million € and 510 million € respectively). "The size of programmes within countries is largely a matter for national discretion, and the product not only of the characteristics of industrial decline in a given country but also the pattern of political forces in operation" (BACHTLER & MICHIE 1996: 723). Clearly, the logic of the framework regulation is not evolving towards a situation where a spatial-economic area analysis is carried out before a region is put forward and (in cases of acceptance by the Commission) before an operational program is drawn up and implemented.

The pattern of Objective 5b regions has become less complex than the Objective 2 regions, although here too the criteria leave room for political tinkering. The basic

---

[8] Unlike the other objective areas, the programming for Objective 2 areas has been broken up into two periods: 1994 –1996 and 1997 – 1999.

criterion is that 5b regions must concern rural areas with a low level of socioeconomic development – as measured by GDP per capita and using the Community average as a gauge. Moreover, the areas must satisfy at least two of the following three criteria:

- a high share of agricultural employment in total employment
- a low level of agricultural income, particularly as expressed in terms of agricultural value added per agricultural work unit (AWU)
- low population density and/or a significant depopulation trend.

The member states are also given the option of putting forward zones that satisfy the basic criteria, and one or more other criteria, such as pressures exerted on the environment and on the countryside.

Here too, the criteria give ample opportunity to shift borders around until an area is created which will, in principle, qualify for a subsidy. One example is the Grampian Region in Scotland that in 1993 (the time when the designation took place) ranked among the top-twenty richest European regions because the oil-producing city Aberdeen lays within its borders. In a display of statistical prowess, the GDP was first calculated at the level of postal codes and then an area was selected which neatly excluded Aberdeen and its environs. The area finally put forward by the British government was selected for funding by the Commission (see Greenwood et al 1995).

When one looks to the designation of areas and the funding decisions in practice, it is not surprising that one of the aims of the 1988 Structural Funds revision has not succeeded, namely concentration, particularly spatial concentration. While only 45% of the population in the European Union fell under region-specific objectives in the 1989 – 1993 period, this increased to over 50% in the current period (see Table 1). In fact, more than half of the EU's population now lives in areas which have the official status of being underprivileged. One of the aims of the new framework regulation for the coming period was to reduce this figure. As was indicated above, the Objective 1 criterion has been sharpened. With regard to the new Objective 2 regions, basically a combination of the former Objective 2 and Objective 5b regions, the new framework regulation has placed a ceiling on the number of residents. According to the framework, the population in all Objective 2 regions should not exceed 18% of the total population of the Community, a decrease of over 7% with regard to the present program period. The Commission will set a different ceiling for each member state. Nevertheless, the current geographic division will linger on into the next period. All regions which had Objective 1, 2 or 5b status in 1999 but which are not selected in the new program period will be eligible for transitional support. The Dutch province of Flevoland, for example, will loose its Objective 1 status, but will receive a transitional budget for the 2000 – 2005 period of over 80% of its current funding.

Table 1 Share of EU population falling under the regional objectives in the 1994 – 1999 period

	Share of Structural Funds	Share of EU Population
Objective 1	68.5%	26.6%
Objective 2	11.0%	16.4%
Objective 5b	5.0%	8.8%
Objective 6	0.5%	0.4%

Source: EUROPEAN COMMISSION 1996, pp. 90-91.

3. Synergy between EU regional policy and Dutch spatial-economic policy

In terms of its share in the Structural Funds budget for the 1994 – 1999 period, the Netherlands ranks among the smaller member states of the European Union. It receives 2.5 billion €, including the horizontal objectives and community initiatives. However, the average annual budget shot up by 167.5% from the previous period – the sharpest increase in the EU (calculation based on EUROPEAN COMMISSION 1996). Another striking statistic is the rise in the share of the Dutch population falling under the Structural Funds' regional objectives. This figure was 12.9% in the 1989 – 1993 period, but grew to 24.1% for the current period[9]. This is quite remarkable given the shift in the objectives and instruments of regional policy in the Netherlands. Present EU cohesion policies are strongly reminiscent of Dutch economic policy of the 1970s. At that time, substantial budgets were allotted for various categories of regions. The 1980s brought with it an awareness that the most serious economic problems actually occurred in the big cities in the core area of the Netherlands, the Randstad. Formal government policy then abandoned its goal of redistributing economic development and replaced it with a policy of bolstering the spatial-economic structure of the country as a whole. At the beginning of the 1990s, the shift in policy from a "geographically-balanced pattern of economic activity" to maximizing the "contribution of the regions to national economic growth" was complete (KLEYN and OOSTERWIJK 1992: 414-415): "In contrast to the classical policy instruments, the new approach is not restricted to areas with a weak regional structure" (ibid.). The framework for this important policy shift has been provided by national spatial planning policy as well as economic policy. One implication of this was to make the term "regional-economic policy" obsolete. The term was still in official use in the period before 1994, but was replaced by spatial-economic policy in 1995. While the European regional stimulation policy enjoyed swelling budgets and extended geographic reach during the 1989 – 1999 period, exactly the opposite occurred in the Netherlands. The most substantial difference between Dutch national policy and that of Europe is the fact that while European policy in the Netherlands is aimed at weak areas, Dutch national policy is mainly geared towards enhancing the spatial-economic structure by targeting high-potential areas. Furthermore, the most significant European program is directed towards one area, Flevoland, which has *no priority whatsoever* in Dutch policy.

---

[9] In the next program period (2000 – 2006) about 15% of the population will fall under the regional objectives of the Structural Funds (excluding transition support).

This contribution will focus on the relationship between spatial planning and the workings of European regional policy in the Netherlands. The analysis to follow is based on a study commissioned by the Netherlands Scientific Council for Government Policy which examined two cases of EU regional policy: the Objective 1 region of the province of Flevoland and the Objective 5b region Friesland. Here mainly the findings of the Flevoland case will be discussed, but references to the Friesland case will be made when applicable. The methodology of the case study is as follows. First, it will be discussed whether the regional policy program matches national and provincial policy, specifically spatial planning policy. The correspondence between European policy programs and that conducted in the Netherlands will be described in terms of synergy. It is assumed that if various policy arenas correspond well, the effectiveness of each separate policy domain will be more than if this had not been the case.

In addition to evaluating the level of synergy between the European regional policy programs and relevant national and provincial level policies, it will be investigated whether synergy exists within EU policy itself. One aim of region-specific policy coordination, as it has been developed within Dutch spatial planning, is to coordinate various "policy pillars." Is this relatively successful within objective regions? This analysis closes with a look to the way in which projects are evaluated within a program. In particular, it will be examined whether spatial planning policy is taken seriously in project procedures.

4. The Flevoland case

4.1 Synergy with current national and provincial policies

The fact that Flevoland received the status of an Objective 1 region raised more than a few eyebrows, especially in the Netherlands. The general sentiment was that the Dutch government had done all it could to get development funds channeled into the Netherlands, funds that were actually meant for the genuinely "poor" regions. This made the Netherlands the only country in the EU where the bestowal of Objective 1 status was met with resistance. The Dutch also have little hesitation about crucifying their own country, even for an international audience. However, this reaction seems misplaced when one looks to the logic behind the selection process of Structural Funds objective regions. According to the rules in force before the 1994 – 1999 period, a region is eligible for Objective 1 status if, for three consecutive years, the per capita GDP is 75% or less than the Community average. It is important to note that this relates to the income generated in the region itself, and not disposable income (as indicated in the new Framework Regulation). 1993 was the year that it had to be determined which regions could be eligible for Objective 1 status for the 1994 – 1999 period. Figures provided at the end of 1992 by Eurostat showed that the GDP for the 1989 – 1991 period in Flevoland lay below 70% of the Community average. It seemed that Objective 1 status was for the taking once the Dutch government put forward the province to the Commission. Once at the Commission, however, the proposal was met with skepticism – some argued that Objective 1 was actually intended for other kinds of regions. Even some ministers within the Dutch government felt that this proposal was inappropriate for these reasons. Nevertheless, it was decided to put forward Flevoland anyway, partially because the 1992 European Council of Edinburgh found that the Netherlands would become a net-payer in the EU, and it was felt that this disparity could be brought back in balance by acquiring a larger piece of the pie via the Structural Funds. Brussels remained unconvinced – that is, until the Dutch government threatened to veto the European Commission's plan for the allocation of Structural Funds altogether (ZONNEVELD & MARTIN 1995: 115). Finally, in 1994, Flevoland became one of the last regions in Europe to be added to the list of Objective 1 regions (RESEARCH VOOR BELEID 1997: 49). The funds made available (150 million €) amounted to "only" half of what was expected (PROVINCIE FLEVOLAND 1993: 11). Initially, the province of Groningen was also being considered as a potential Objective 1 region. Since Groningen has a long history of aid within the context of Dutch regional policy, conferring Objective 1 status to this area would correspond very well to national policy. However, this initiative failed due to natural gas profits which, according to the logic of the Framework Regulation, must be counted as income. Dutch arguments that one should look at the per capita income within the region and not regional GDP per capita proved irrelevant for the formal criteria for designating Objective 1 regions. In the end, part of northwestern Groningen was awarded the status of an Objective 5b region.

It must be concluded that while the designation of Flevoland as an Objective 1 region is in complete accordance with the letter of the Structural Funds' Framework Regulation, it is still hard to reconcile with the spirit of this document. Furthermore, as previously stated, the selection of Flevoland as an Objective 1 region has absolutely no connection to current national policy, direct or indirect. On the other hand, the selection certainly does not conflict with this policy. In this sense, the conclusion which can be read in the single programming document for Flevoland is not entirely true: that the Objective 1 program is completely in line with present and past Dutch national policy (EUROPEAN COMMISSION 1996: 11).

The main point that needs to be made here is that the designation of regions should be done within a framework which defines the economic well-being of the region not only in terms of affluence but also in terms of this region's position within the spatial-economic structure. Seen this way, the fact that the designation of regions in Dutch spatial-economic policy produces a different result than European regional policy is striking. It must be concluded that, to put it lightly, there is a lack of synergy between Dutch national policy regarding the spatial-economic structure and European regional policy. At lower levels of scale (i.e. the objective regions themselves) this is much less apparent.

When, during the course of 1993, it became clear that Flevoland would receive an Objective 1 status, a Regional Development Program (*Regionaal Ontwikkelingsprogramma: ROP*) was quickly drawn up as a first step towards the final policy program to be established as an SPD. Given European objective-region practices, it was no easy task to formulate an internally coherent policy program which was also consistent with current national government policy and with the various local governments and other stakeholders involved. However, the drafters of Flevoland's ROP benefited from the fact that the provincial regional plan had recently been adopted (March 3, 1993) and that two other important plans – the Environmental Policy Plan and the Water Management Plan – were nearly rounded off. In general, this resulted in a large degree of coherence between the ROP and other areas of provincial policy. This is very similar to the situation in Friesland in which the provincial plan (and other policy frames) supported the drawing up of the development program.

The national government played only a nominal role in the formulation of the ROP, published in October 1993. Those involved described the ROP as a pure "Flevoland product". The projects identified were borrowed from the available provincial plans and draft plans. In addition, the policy priorities that should precede these according to the Brussels method, were also written in view of these projects.

The ROP was later modified on a number of points in negotiations with the Commission. Observers indicated that the Commission was very concerned about the faithful application of European regulations, especially environmental policy regulations. A substantive appraisal of spatial impacts was not carried out as the province of Flevoland generally does this using its own planning frameworks.

During the formulation of the SPD, the Commission followed standard procedure and did not advance its own preferences at the project level. However, this was not the case for the policy priorities, and the Commission insisted that a policy priority regarding the fishing sector be included. The subsidy involved (the Financial Instrument for Fisheries Guidance) was still relatively new and evidently the Commission wished to apply the FIFG in Flevoland to show that it was needed. Meanwhile it has been shown that the added value of this instrument for Flevoland (the village of Urk in this case) was relatively minor. The FIFG instrument can only be employed for measures which relate directly to the fishing sector (e.g. investments in fish/aqua cultures). However, the decline in fish quotas increased calls for expanding the economic basis of Urk (RESEARCH VOOR BELEID 1997: 27). The FIFG instrument does not allow for this kind of "ERDF-ish" approach however. Although certainly no inconsistency exists between the Objective 1 program for Flevoland and its own provincial policy, no synergy exists either – although EU structural policy does formally strive towards this.

4.2 Synergy within european policy

European structural policy aims to achieve synergy between its policy measures. Therefore, there should be synergy within the Objective 1 program for Flevoland (see below). Synergy should also exist between this program and other European policies. To begin with the latter: at least five Community Initiatives are underway in Flevoland with a total budget of over 12.5 million €. Two of these relate to region-specific programs (LEADER II and PESCA), and the others relate to national programs which channel these resources to Flevoland (SMEs, Employment, ADAPT). The ongoing evaluation of the SPD mentioned that the large number of funds active in Flevoland "sometimes" caused tension between the various programs. If different funds are targeted towards the same groups within a single area, this can threaten the added value of the various European programs. Problems can also arise in finding the required co-financing, as many parties attempt to extract funds from the same source. This is especially true for the SME and LEADER II initiatives (RESEARCH VOOR BELEID

1997: 62-63). One can thus question the level of synergy achieved between the various European programs.

As was the case for the Objective 5b region in Friesland, it was the agencies involved in the implementation of the SPD program that ensured that a certain degree of integration took place between the European programs. The Community Initiatives were carried out by the SPD Flevoland project management team. The Commission did not take the initiative for arriving at a good integration of the European programs; this had to happen from the bottom-up in the region concerned (Flevoland).

Flevoland's program has a fairly complicated structure: a total of 53 measures are identified within eight priority categories (moreover eight measures are split up into two or three sub-categories; if these are also counted the total is 64). The SPD structure is even more complex than the ROP's (which had five "priority topics" divided into eighteen "programs" in total). This program was drawn up in the expectation that 300 million € would be made available. Because of this, the Brussels principle of concentrating resources into a limited number of activities had lost much of its meaning (RESEARCH VOOR BELEID 1997: 35). There are other objections. First, the large number of measures make the programs less flexible as money may only be transferred from one priority to another within certain set parameters. Larger transfers require the consent of the Commission, which takes at least four months (ibid. 37). Second, the large number of measures is not conducive to the internal cohesion of the program (ibid. 35). Measures overlap and, more importantly, are only marginally coordinated[10]. We can conclude that there is evidence of a lack of cohesion between the various measures. That one can still find this cohesion at the level of concrete actions can largely be attributed to the fact that policy frames at the provincial level – more than the SPD itself – are used to frame the decision-making process on projects, according to various spokesmen. Referring back to the beginning of this paper: the 1988 revision of the Structural Funds was geared towards increasing the synergy between the three funds. To do this, an organizational division was made within the project management of the various funds in the SPDs for all EU region-specific programs (including Objective 2 and 5b programs) in the Netherlands, like Flevoland. The Ministry of Social Affairs and Employment specifically charged the Regional Employment Council (*Regionaal Beraad voor de Arbeidsvoorziening: RBA*) with the project management of the 40 million € ESF funds. These funds are spent within a separate organization according to its own procedure. The other funds (ERDF, EAGGF, FIFG) have a single project management body. Coordination talks take place at the administrative level between the RBA on the one hand, and the steering committee (*stuurgroep*) for the other funds on the other (i.e. the Provincial Executive: the *College van Gedeputeerde Staten*). The total program falls under the responsibility of the Supervisory Commission.

Although the parties involved in the Flevoland program were unable to name any serious bottlenecks between the two project management organizations, the construction as a whole was still considered disadvantageous. The division can lead to coordination

---

[10] The ongoing evaluation recommends a substantial reduction in the number of regulations. Shifting the priorities of the program is not recommended (RESEARCH VOOR BELEID, 1997, 38).

problems, and the existence of multiple "desks" can cause confusion for the target groups (RESEARCH VOOR BELEID 1997: 42). The Flevoland parties also felt that the acting European directorate-generals interacted as "sovereign kingdoms," each with their own approval procedures and administrative processes (e.g. separate forms for each of the funds). The Supervisory Commission was viewed as being fairly powerless in this respect. All in all, the parties agreed that synergy between the funds – the goal of the 1988 revision – did not really materialize in Flevoland.

4.3 Project evaluation

The synergy between the SPD for Flevoland and current policy frames is different at different levels of scale. Because one cannot derive a specific economic stimulation policy for Flevoland from national policy frames, and because both are certainly not in conflict, one can describe the synergy with national policy as "neutral". On the other hand, synergy with provincial policy frames is potentially very high. However, this raises a series of questions: how does the SPD work in practice? Is the potential synergy between the SPD and the provincial policy frame apparent in the way in which projects are handled and evaluated? How is this relayed back to the relevant policy frames, including those involving spatial planning? In order to answer these questions, it is important to look at how subsidy applications are evaluated. It must be stressed here that the implementation of an EU program involves installing a specific organizational structure to run alongside existing structures for regular policy. The issue of synergy between EU regional policy in the Netherlands and Dutch provincial policy therefore relates to the link between these structures. Decisions on projects in the framework of the Structural Funds must therefore fit within both an Operational Program – the SPD in the case of Flevoland – as well as within the current policy frames.

The organizational structure of Flevoland's SPD contains the usual three levels: the Supervisory Commission, the Steering Committee, and the Program Management. The composition of the Supervisory Committee adheres closely to the principle of partnership (see Table 2).

At the level of the SPD Steering Committee, the organization of the Flevoland program differs fundamentally from the other objective programs (with the exception of the 5b region Friesland). Normally, the Steering Committee contains a broad group of actors who more or less conform to the composition of the Supervisory Commission. In Flevoland, the SPD Steering Committee consists of only the Administration of the Regional Employment Council and the Provincial Executive.

Although the Supervisory Commission ultimately decides on project proposals, the Provincial Executive plays a key role in the organization of the SPD program. This is a result of the explicit desire to underline the "political-administrative responsibility" of this body in decision-making and providing administrative guidance (COLLEGE VAN GEDEPUTEERDE STATEN FLEVOLAND 1994: 10). A comparable choice was made regarding the substantive evaluation of project proposals at the Program Management level. Although it bears the single name "Program Management" this third level in the organizational structure has two separate parts: ESF fund management (ESF Bureau) and Program Management Europe (PME) for the other funds (ERDF, EAGGF, FIFG). In

Flevoland, it was explicitly decided to have the PME become an integral part of the provincial apparatus. A number of other objective regions have split off the project management from the policy apparatus and delegated it to a semiprivate body. The main reason for this was that subvention for technical assistance could be used from the program budget.

Table 2   Composition of the supervisory committee for the Flevoland Objective 1 program

- European Commission: DG V (Employment, Industrial Relations and Social Affairs); DG VI (Agriculture); DG XIV (Fisheries); DG XVI (Regional Policy and Cohesion)
- European Investment Bank
- The Ministries of: Economic Affairs; Transport, Public Works and Water Management; Agriculture, Nature Management and Fisheries; Ministry of Housing, Spatial Planning and Environment; Ministry of Social Affairs and Employment
- Regional Employment Council (RBA) Flevoland
- Province of Flevoland: the Crown Commissioner (chairman); Provincial Executive
- Local councils (2 representatives)
- Water management authorities (1 representative)
- Flevoland Farmers' Union
- Socioeconomic Consultation and Advisory Council (SEOR)
- Trade union representative
- Chamber of Commerce

Source: EUROPEAN COMMISSION 1996B; RESEARCH VOOR BELEID 1997: 40

Examining the way in which project proposals are submitted in the Flevoland program will reveal a direct connection between provincial policies (at least those concerning non-ESF funds). The various provincial agencies – such as Spatial Planning and Housing – play a key role in the substantive evaluation of the project proposals. The heads of these departments are brought together into a steering group for Europe (*Stuurgroep Europa*), which, due to its lack of an official place in the organizational structure (RESEARCH VOOR BELEID 1997: 43), should not be confused with the SPD Steering Committee. Despite this, the most important decisions on the actual content of the program are taken by the agencies themselves. It can be concluded that this *modus operandi* largely guarantees that projects will conform to provincial policy, including spatial planning policy. Specifically, spatially relevant project proposals are evaluated in part by using the Provincial Regional Plan as a framework.

5. Conclusions and implications

Policy concerning Objective 1, 2, and 5b regions is highly spatially significant. Despite this fact, the selection of these areas is carried out in a way that bears no resemblance to sensible spatial policy. When areas are put forward by member states, no consideration is given to spatial visions of the national territory, nor the position or role which the objective region would fulfill within that territory. In fact, the logic behind the criteria in the framework regulation for the European Structural Funds does not even allow for this. Moreover, the ultimate selection and delineation of objective regions by the European Commission is devoid of any vision of the desired spatial structure of the European Union. Consequently, any similarity between objective regions and spatial strategies is most likely coincidental.

Of course, one can argue that the picture created by the designated objective regions carries some sort of implicit vision of the European Union's territory. Even if this were the case, such a vision is not based on imagery regarding the unique spatial or geo-economic features of this European territory. The pattern of objective regions is so splintered and incoherent that the existence of a spatial vision is out of the question. Given that spatial policy lacks legal treaty status, one cannot make an appeal to the principles articulated in the treaty. The European Spatial Development Perspective, adopted in Potsdam May 1999 (EUROPEAN COMMISSION 1999), could function as guide regarding the question of where the Structural Funds could be applied with priority. However, because this policy lacks a formal (treaty) status, how this would be done in practice is another question entirely. The southern member states are very apprehensive about allowing the ESDP to perform this role. The criteria that is currently being used to allocate budgets has led to a situation where these member states are generally eligible for Structural Funds. Each possible shift – whether to the North or the East (i.e. new EU member states) – will be met with resistance from the cohesion countries, especially Spain. On the other hand, it was precisely this that the initiators of the ESDP, especially Germany, had in mind: to let the ESDP serve as a basis for allocating Structural Funds. Discussions about net-payers and net-receivers in the fall of 1997, sparked off by Germany and the Netherlands (both proponents of European cooperation in spatial planning), will however result in keeping the ESDP subordinate to distribution politics.

When one looks to how the Structural Funds work in the Netherlands, it is striking to see how little influence Dutch national spatial planning seems to have on regional programs supported by structural fund subsidies. Even though this is so important in a spatial sense, the criteria by which regions are defined and selected simply do not allow for this. Indeed, the status of national spatial planning has been fairly marginalized in this regard. This situation is not much better in other policy areas. The method of setting priorities at the European level is consistent with Dutch regional-economic policy twenty years ago that targeted socio-economically disadvantaged regions.

The designation of Flevoland as an Objective 1 region is clearly not the result of some sort of spatial or spatial-economic analysis, including SWOT analyses. If we look to the policy program as established in the Single Programming Document, then it is not surprising that a clear focus is absent. In fact, one can hardly call it a plan at all. In a plan, a close relationship exists between a situational analysis of the area in question and the identification of problems and the concrete actions needed to solve these (c.f. BUUNK, HETSEN & JANSEN 1999). In this light, it is interesting to note the connections between the organizational structure of the Objective 1 program and the current administrative organization at the provincial level. It is striking to see how much current provincial policy frames (especially the regional plan) were used when drawing up the SPD for Flevoland. These frames also play a crucial part in the evaluation and selection of projects. It is largely thanks to this that some synergy can be found within the European policy, although this remains rather limited in spite of the Structural Funds revision. It is also at the regional level that synergy arises between the regional programs and European regulations, and European policy falling outside the workings of the SPD. Similar conclusions can be drawn regarding the policy for the most important 5b program (Friesland).

In the Friesland case, no coherent spatial-economic development strategy could be guaranteed via the organizational principle of partnership. Some sort of planning was necessary. In the Netherlands, a coherent system of plans is in place in various policy areas and at various scales. Spatial plans play a key role in this system. These were utilized at the provincial level when applying for and drawing up EU regional policy programs. When such plans are absent, they must be drafted by the many involved parties. The problem remains that although regional policy can be characterized as a form of spatial policy, no spatial framework exists at the European level for the selection and delineation of regions. At present, the European Spatial Development Perspective cannot fill this gap, as it still lacks a formal status. Moreover, the content of this document still lies too much at the level of global objectives and policy aims to offer real guidance at the level of concrete areas. No spatial indicators are available to replace the eligibility criteria of the Framework Regulation. There is an awareness, especially within the Commission, that this situation has to change. The entry of new member states in the European Union will result in a considerable reduction in the EU's average GDP. Regions with a per capita GDP considerably below the Community average is currently decisive for qualifying for the Structural Funds, especially in the case of the Objective 1 regions, which receive by far the largest portion of the Structural Funds. Simple mathematics show that once the community average drops as the result of the accession of new Central and Eastern European member states many, or even nearly all of the regions currently enjoying structural fund subsidies will lose their eligibility. This is politically volatile – not to mention the myriad budget problems that will arise if the present allocation system is maintained. So we are looking at what may possibly be the greatest overhaul of the Structural Funds since 1975. A search will ensue for new allocation criteria, criteria which could well be of a spatial character. The study program on European spatial planning (SPESP) – which is currently being carried out by a network of national research institutes and which is in its first stage of development – largely aims to offer a package of spatial indicators which could serve as new allocation criteria. These indicators were mentioned in the first full draft of the European Spatial Development Perspective of 1997 (EUROPEAN COMMISSION 1997). They are geographical position, economic strength, social integration, spatial integration, land-use pressure, cultural assets, and natural assets. The basic assumption is that these indicators could give a clear picture of the spatial differentiation in the present and future European Union and thus could serve as a base for defining policy measures at all levels of scale. The search is on for simple ways to make these indicators operational. Each indicator should be transparent in its subject matter, otherwise policymakers will not accept these as an "objective" base for decision-making. This research program should also make it clear that each indicator raises relevant policy issues and that this legitimizes its use in decision-making.

This is no easy task; especially considering the fact that a host of national research institutes with professionals from various backgrounds and cultures are now struggling to reach a common understanding. The result should be available in 2004 when the discussions for the new budget period commence. Considering the geological timescale at which policy and institutional changes usually take place in the European Union, this is a very short period indeed.

Bibliography

BACHTLER, J. & R. MICHIE (1993): "The Restructuring of Regional Policy in the European Community", Regional Studies, Vol. 27, No. 8, pp. 719-725.

BASTRUP-BIRK, H. & P. DOUCET (1997): "European Spatial Planning from the Heart", Built Environment: Special Issue: Shaping Europe: The European Spatial Development Perspective, Vol. 23, No. 4, pp. 307-314.

BRUINSMA, W. (1996): "EZ en Europese regionale programma's in Nederland", Osmose; Kwartaalmonitor van de Stichting Maatschappij en Onderneming, Jg. 22, No. 1, p.14-15.

BUUNK, W., H. HETSEN & A.J. JANSEN (1999): "From sectoral to regional policies: a first step towards spatial planning in the European Union?", European Planning Studies, Vol. 7, No. 1, pp. 81-98.

COLLEGE VAN GEDEPUTEERDE STATEN FLEVOLAND (1994): "Interne organisatie uitvoering Regionaal Ontwikkelingsplan Flevoland 1994 – 1999", In: Provincie Flevoland - Administratieve organisatie programma management Europa; Bijlage 1, p.10-17, Lelystad: Provincie Flevoland.

CORBETT, R., F. JACOBS & M. SHACKLETON (1995): The European Parliament, London: Catermill Publishing.

EUROPEAN COMMISSION (1996): First Report on Economic and Social Cohesion 1996, Luxembourg: Office for Official Publications of the European Communities.

EUROPEAN COMMISSION (1997): European Spatial Development Perspective: First Official Draft; Presented at the Informal Meeting of Ministers Responsible for Spatial Planning of the Member States of the European Union, Noordwijk, June 1997, Luxembourg: Office for Official Publications of the European Communities.

EUROPEAN COMMISSION (1999): European Spatial Development Perspective; Towards Balanced and Sustainable Development of the Territory of the European Union, Luxembourg: Office for Official Publications of the European Communities

EUROPESE COMMISSIE (1996): Flevoland – Gecombineerd programmeringsdocument 1994 – 1999; Doelstelling 1: Structurele ontwikkeling en aanpassing van regio's met een ontwikkelingsachterstand; Document, Luxemburg: Bureau voor officiële publikaties der Europese Gemeenschappen.

GREENWOOD, J., R. LEVY & R. STEWART (1995): "The European Union Structural Fund allocations: lobbying to win or recycling the budget?", European Urban and Regional Studies, pp. 317-338.

KLEYN, W.H. & J.W. OOSTERWIJK (1992): "Regional Impact and Policy Responses to the Single European Market: The Dutch Perspective", Regional Studies, Vol.26, No. 4, pp. 411-416.

LIPIETZ, A. (1995): "Avoiding megapolization: The Battle of Ile-de-France", in: European Planning Studies, Vol. 3, No. 2, p. 143-154.

MARTIN, D. & H. TEN VELDEN (1997): "Extra Options as Optional Extras: What Ideas are behind the ESDP?", Built Environment: Special Issue: Shaping Europe: The European Spatial Development Perspective, Vol. 23, No. 4, pp. 267-280.

MINEKUS, H.D. (1994): "De casus Flevoland: een geslaagde Eurolobby?", Openbaar Bestuur, Jg. 4, No. 11, p. 11-14.

NUGENT, N. (1999): The Government and Politics of the European Union (4th edn), Basingstoke: Macmillan.

PROVINCIE FLEVOLAND (1993): Flevoland, naar een gemeenschappelijke ontwikkeling van een nieuwe regio; Regionaal Ontwikkelingsplan voor de periode 1994 – 1999, Lelystad: Provincie Flevoland.

RESEARCH VOOR BELEID (1997): On going evaluatie Doelstelling 1 programma Flevoland, Leiden: Research voor Beleid.

SCHOBBEN, R.J.P. (1995): "De regionale bestuurslaag in Nederland en elders in Europa: een vergelijkende analyse", Bestuurswetenschappen, Jg. 49, No. 5, p. 351-372.

WILLIAMS, R.H. (1996): European Union Spatial Policy and Planning, London: Paul Chapman Publishing.

ZONNEVELD W. & A. FALUDI (1998): Europese integratie en de Nederlandse ruimtelijke ordening, Voorstudies en achtergronden Wetenschappelijke Raad voor het Regeringsbeleid V102, Den Haag: Sdu Uitgevers.

ZONNEVELD, W. & D. MARTIN, D. (1995): "Nieuwe initiatieven voor de ruimtelijke ordening in Europa", in: ZONNEVELD, W. & F. EVERS (red.) Europa op de plankaart, 113-118, Den Haag: Nederlands Instituut voor Ruimtelijke Ordening en Volkshuisvesting-Europlan.

"Regions of the Future" – Sustainable Development through Cooperation and Competition

THORSTEN WIECHMANN

1. Introduction

In September 1997 the Federal Ministry for Regional Planning, Building and Urban Development (now: Federal Ministry of Transport, Construction and Housing / *Bundesministerium für Verkehr, Bau- und Wohnungswesen, BMVBW*) announced the "Regions of the Future" competition[1]. The competition left territorial boundaries and organizational constitution up to the regions. Special emphasis was given to processes of dialogue and cooperation between representatives of the population and interest groups. During May 1998, 26 regions were selected by a jury and awarded the rating "Region of the Future – Moving Towards Sustainable Development". In the following months these regions had to work out regional Agenda 21 schemes for sustainable spatial and settlement development. The last phase of the competition – the implementation phase – started in May 1999.

This paper will focus on explaining the concept behind this competition and looks at its realization as what it is hoped will be 'good practice' in regional development in Germany and Europe.

While primarily a German initiative with a solely national dimension, the problems underpinning it – the unsustainability of modern societies and the destruction of our natural resources – are of course global. Thus it has also been lent a European dimension.

Accordingly, the objective of this paper is to provide a brief overview of the idea of the "Regions of the Future" competition in the context of sustainable regional development. The concluding remarks will focus on two main questions: How important for problem solving and development in European regions is the rediscovery of processes of dialogue and cooperationwith a "bottom-up approach"? And: How appropriate are competitions as a new type of instrument (in Germany at least) for spatial and regional policies?

2. The German "Regions of the Future" competition: idea and realization

After local authorities, regions are one of the most important players in the movement towards sustainable development worldwide. Initiatives that mesh local approaches – such as Local Agenda 21 – with regional strategies are becoming increasingly important. This is because problems such as intensive land-use or changes in resource supplies and waste flows do not stop at the borders of municipalities. If effective pol-

---

[1] For further details on the "Regions of the Future" competition see BBR 1997, BBR 1998, BBR 1999, Adam 1998, Adam / Wiechmann 1999 a) and the website for the competition: http://www.zukunftsregionen.de/

icy decisions and regulations for the long-term well-being of citizens are to be found, cooperation and coordination between neighboring local authorities will become essential (ICLEI 1999).

2.1 Starting point Agenda 21

The Earth Summit, held in Rio de Janeiro in 1992, opened up an international dialogue on sustainable development at the global level. At this UN Conference for Environment and Development (UNCED) it was decided to set in motion a global action plan dubbed 'Agenda 21'. The "Regions of the Future" competition can be understood as a practically orientated project forming part of this plan.

"Agenda 21"

The final paper of the Rio conference in 1992, the 'Agenda 21' document, maps out the foundations for sustainable development – a form of development that addresses economic, social and ecological concerns and brings them together on an equal footing. In Chapter 28 of this agenda for the 21st century, local authorities are urged to enter into dialogue with their citizens and to actively take part in the drawing up of local agendas and their implementation. It is a call that has been heeded with positive results in many places. The decision has already been made to draw up a "Local Agenda 21" in over 500 German municipalities.

There are a lot of questions regarding implementation of the agenda at municipal level, however: Which role does the regional level actually play in sustainable development? How are relevant players to be motivated to engage in sustainable development? How can appropriate strategies of action and institutional structures for the development and conversion of regional agendas be found?

These questions are the starting point for the "Regions of the Future" competition, which – as an answer to these thematic questions – will support the drawing up and effectuation of regional agendas for sustainable spatial and settlement development.

2.2 Aim of the competition

The overall aim of the competition is sustainable regional development. The development of German and European regions should be directed towards sustainability.

Concerning the building up of self-supporting structures for sustainable development, reciprocal learning is a further fundamental objective of the competition.

Overall, the competition itself is less important than cooperation between those active in the regions. Nevertheless, it is designed to lead to an intensive exchange of experience, giving regions the chance to learn from each other.

2.3 Tasks of the regions

The development strategy of a region should aim at satisfying the needs of the current generation without compromising the possibility for future generations to satisfy their needs. Strategies should be devised to harmonize social and economic demands with the environmental capacity of an area.

In fact, the main task of the regions lies in setting a course for sustainable regional development through regional planning. With this 'aim for the future' in mind, the regions taking part in the competition are to get innovations off the drawing board and see that the projects and ideas are put into action. By the end of the competition in July 2000 the regions are to have tackled two different tasks:

1. They are to implement projects for sustainable development or present project ideas that could be implemented in the short or medium term. These projects can then serve as examples for other regions. Popular items are projects and drafts conducive, for example, to comparatively low-traffic types of land-use and better protection of open land as well as a more efficient flow of materials and energy or the support of innovative, ecologically driven enterprises.

2. They are required to set a course for sustainable spatial and settlement development by building self-supporting structures.

Special emphasis is placed on processes of dialogue and cooperation with representatives of the population and interest groups.

2.4 Course of the competition

2.4.1 Entries

The former BfLR (the Federal Research Institute of Geography and Regional Planning, today part of the Federal Office for Building and Regional Planning – BBR) launched this competition on September 11, 1997. About 130 regions from all parts of Germany, among them some cross-border regions, enrolled for this competition within the period of registration ending on November 7, 1997. 87 of these regions handed in their applications by the deadline of January 31, 1998. Each region set out its aims, strategies and projects for sustainable spatial and settlement development in its entry documents. These were often a first concept for a 'Regional Agenda 21'. Prior to enrolment the regions had to qualify in an application procedure.

2.4.2 Selection of entrants

A jury of experts selected 26 regions from those entered in the course of May 1998. At the inaugural event in Würzburg in June 1998, these regions were awarded the rating "Regions of the Future – Moving Towards Sustainable Development" by the Federal Minister for Building at that time, Mr. EDUARD OSWALD.

The BfLR formulated four main criteria of assessment in its invitation for entries (BFLR 1997). These were to serve to guarantee a transparent as well as a comprehensive assessment of entry documents.

1. There is a willingness for dialogue and cooperation at regional level.

    For sustainable regional development to be implemented, the various local players in a region must be engaged in a dialogue with one another. Among the most basic requirements is the dialogue between local authorities within the region and regional planning authorities. The local population should also be directly involved in both the planning and implementation of concrete measures with regional implications. Ideas for a Regional Agenda 21 may be developed out of Local Agenda 21 processes. With the help of such dialogue, people's awareness of sustainability issues can be awakened or reinforced. Additionally, dialogue between local authorities will pave the way for consensus on decisions and agreements concerning sustainable regional development.

2. The region is defined by common problems and potential.

The region to be considered should represent an area delimited by particular, defined problems and solutions. For example, a region may be delimited by the infrastructural relationships of settlements, interdependent local economies, or shared or overlapping supply or waste flows. Local government units within the defined region should have shared approaches to problem-solving and to developing the future potential of the area.

3. Many innovative, complementary strategies and projects are to be expected.

The many projects currently underway in a region should be expected to yield long-term ecological, social and economic benefits. To this end, it is essential that projects and strategies within different thematic areas be integrated around common goals.

Once common regional goals are established, diverse projects and strategies may have a complementary or synergetic effect on regional developments. On the other hand, to prevent diverse projects from working against one another, they should be managed together. With the aid of indicators and time-scales, the success and effectiveness of activities may be measured and evaluated.

4. The region has started down the path to sustainable spatial and housing development.

Recognizable beginnings of initiatives that will lead to sustainable regional development should already be apparent. While some regions may already be in the process of implementing projects towards sustainable regional development, other steps along the way may include the development of a conceptual framework outlining starting points for a comprehensive and integrated approach to sustainable development. Projects currently up and running need not necessarily be labeled as "sustainable regional development" to be included in this assessment.

2.4.3 'Competition of Ideas' and 'Competition to Implement'

As already mentioned, in the course of May 1998 26 regions were selected by a jury from 87 entrants and awarded the rating "Region of the Future – Moving Towards Sustainable Development". Apart from the "honor", the region won an offer of professional advice but no funds.

The competition has meanwhile become a combined 'Competition of Ideas' and implementation and will conclude with a presentation of submissions and prize awards at the "URBAN 21" Global Conference on the Future of Cities being held in July 2000 in Berlin. The subdivision of the competition into two phases – 'Competition of Ideas' and 'Competition to Implement' – purely underlines the elements involved and is not a strict division. Accordingly, during the 'Competition of Ideas' it is already possible to put single projects to effect (especially in view of the short term of the competition). Concerning the Competition to Implement, openness for new ideas is demanded.

By May 1999, the selected regions had to have drawn up (in the context of the 'Competition of Ideas') regional Agenda 21 schemes for sustainable spatial and settlement development. For this task and for the subsequent implementation phase, the regions were supported by the Federal Office for Building and Regional Planning (BBR) and further institutions.

Participants in the competition are professionally involved in relevant regional fields of action such as

- economy and work,
- flows of materials and energy,
- land use and settlement development,
- transport infrastructure
- education and culture, and
- tourism.

Processes of dialogue and cooperations: The Institute for Organizational Communication in Bensheim (IFOK) is organizing and presenting the competition nationally on behalf of the Federal Office for Building and Regional Planning (BBR) and is also a point of intersection for all advisory services relating to the competition. Furthermore, as a professional institute, IFOK offers advice to the regions involved in the competition on aspects of their processes of dialogue and cooperation.

Fields of advice are for example:

- regional organization models
- public-private partnerships
- management of processes in agenda projects
- cooperative development of projects
- methods for resolving conflicts
- financing models
- public relations etc.

Together, BBR and IFOK organize "services" for the professional and communications needs of participants – such as, for example, the documentation of regional "good practices" and their tailoring to the requirements in specific regions. Both organizations also avail themselves of external know-how, in the form of experts for example, so as to enhance the potential for solving both specific and more general regional problems.

Organization and exchanges of experience: this involves a long-term task with a prominent role from the outset. It has the objective of continuously interlinking people, information and projects.

Important instruments in this respect are

- an *Internet homepage* for the competition (http://www.zukunftsregionen.de) with information about the state of progress of the competition, developments in the respective regions, new discoveries and current literature, all of which is available to the professional public in all interested regions

- a regularly published *"competition newspaper"* (also available to the public, see BBR 1998, BBR 1999), which reports on developments in the 26 competition regions, specialist research in the field of sustainable spatial and settlement development etc.

- an *Internet project database* to facilitate exchanges of ideas between competition regions and the supply of information to other regions and the professional public (http://www.zukunftsregionen.de/projektboerse/main.htm)

- the holding of *functions*, specifically 'Innovation Forums' which all 87 original entrants are invited to attend, 'Creativity Workshops' which are reserved for the 26 competition participants, and conferences on special topics.

2.4.4 Final at the URBAN 21 Global Conference

The competition will experience its grand finale at the URBAN 21 Global Conference. This conference is one of the key planks in the Global Initiative on Sustainable Development, sponsored by Brazil, Germany, Singapore and South Africa. URBAN 21 is aimed at all experts involved in the development of towns and cities who support the improvement of living and environmental conditions in urban areas. It is organized by the Federal Ministry of Transport, Construction and Housing (BMVBW) and will take place in Berlin as part of the EXPO World Exhibition 2000 in Hanover.

Clearly, it will not be possible to bring about sustainable development by the deadline of the competition in summer 2000, but signals can be sent out and the course set for the period thereafter. Thus, the final of the competition is simultaneously a point of departure for the broad-based continuation of regional agenda processes in Germany.

2.5 Understanding of sustainability in the competition

Sustainable development signifies a process, which pays attention in equal measure to economic, social and ecological requirements. Moreover and this is crucial, it satisfies the needs of those alive today without depriving future generations of the same opportunity.

The Federal Office for Building and Regional Planning (BBR) has formulated a definition of sustainability for use as a framework for approaches in the regions (BfLR 1997: 3). The following encapsulation of objectives would appear capable of general consensus:

Objectives for sustainable spatial and settlement development

ecological objectives

- restriction of building on open land for settlements
- encouragement of local and regional flows of material and energy
- constraints on use of non-regenerative raw materials and energy resources
- reduction of noxious emissions into the environment

social objectives

- equal participation by and attention to interests of all regional players and population groups

economic objectives

- preservation and creation of regional jobs in innovative, environmentally-oriented enterprises
- consolidation and improvement of effectiveness of public budgets

With due regard to the respective situation, problems and potential, however, these abstract objectives of the "Regions of the Future" need to be adapted to suit sustainable development as well as being complemented in concrete terms.

As often happens, here too the basic consensus in any individual case may be surrendered (ADAM 1999: 5). This is notably the case where a given party has to make sacrifices in the name of sustainable development without being able to expect any compensatory equivalent. Such a constellation of conflicts may, for example, arise when

- a municipality has to decide whether the locating of companies and jobs is threatened, and could perhaps be lost to another municipality, owing to environmental concerns relating to the site(s) involved
- the use of public transport is more sustainable than driving your own car, but for the individual this does not seem to be advantageous or to have any tangible benefit

The competition entitled "Regions of the Future - Regional Agendas for Sustainable Area and Settlement Development" has the aim of developing or extending possible solutions to conflicts so as to more effectively square ecological, social and economic, but also individual interests. This is to be reached through

- encouragement and supply of planning creativity
- negotiation and mediation of different interests
- search for appropriate constellations of instruments.

The regional dimension

The regional dimension has been the central focus in much debate on sustainable development – but why is this? Is it simply because taking action in regional matters has become fashionable in many ways in recent years? The general increase in the significance of this regional dimension has supposedly taken the debate on sustainable regional development and regional agendas further forward. If one looks at the matter in greater detail, it is indeed evident that regional efforts to implement sustainable development carry far greater weight than action at the municipal level – at least from a regional planning point of view (ADAM 1999: 6).

First and foremost, this significance is traceable to the fact that many environmental, social and economic problems associated with sustainable development can no longer be solved within municipalities and much of the potential within sustainable development cannot be tapped by a city or community 'going it alone'. Where individual municipalities reach the end of their tether, scope for regional action emerges.

Important preliminary tasks of the competition related, on the one hand, to analyzing such limits to municipal action and, on the other, to assessing – hypothetically in the first instance – complementary potential attainable through inter-municipal and regional endeavors (ADAM/BLACH 1997). From these preliminary examinations it follows that regional moves play a key part in the implementation of sustainable spatial and settlement development. It was possible to demonstrate and illustrate the regional scope for action with respect to regional and settlement development, transport infrastructure and flows of material and energy.

2.6 Structure of "Regions of the Future"

The map of the 26 competitors reveals that the regions differ discernibly in size (Figure 1). Some correspond to established German planning regions or to rural districts, others have been defined on the basis of physical features (low mountain ranges, catchment areas of rivers). There are additionally two cross-border regions: the German-Dutch EUREGIO and the Franco-German cooperation area christened PAMINA. The number of inhabitants varies from 4 million in the Metropolitan Region of Hamburg to 69,000 in the Aller/Leine Valley. Surface area ranges from 18,842 km² in the Metropolitan Region of Hamburg to 441 km² in South Leipzig District.

The competition regions also differ with respect to their coordinators – these being, variously, rural districts, regional planning authorities, intermunicipal cooperative entities or, indeed, private institutions that opt to run a network project. This diversity is the outcome of the openness of the competition, which was targeted not only at administrative regions but also at self-organized parts thereof as well as at public or privately supported regional initiatives. In other words, both spatial delimitation and organizational structure are variable.

An appraisal of all 87 regions that entered the competition is likewise illuminating, since it indicates the spatial borders within which such regional agenda processes are likely to arise on a voluntary basis and which players tend to be involved. An analysis of entry documents shows the following:

1. Entries generally reflect the regional variety found in Germany. Comprising 31 of the 87 regions entered for the competition, the new federal states (*"Länder"*) in eastern Germany are significantly represented. 8 of the selected regions are situated in rural areas, 8 in agglomeration areas, another 5 each in urban regions and the hinterland of big cities.

2. Associations, initiatives, teams or private companies – in some cases together with a planning association – are the biggest group of entrants, having submitted 36 of the 87 applications. In 9 cases regional planning associations were solely responsible, in 12 more cases they cooperated with other parties. Even more frequent are forms of cooperation between municipalities and rural districts acting as coordinators within the competition (26 entries). This finding underlines the variety of possible initiators of agenda processes at the regional level (WIECHMANN 1999).

3. In their entries, regions declared their main focus as being topics such as general regional development and settlement development (45) and economy and work (40).

2.7 Projects within "Regions of the Future"

The range of projects in the "Regions of the Future" will now be exemplified using 3 arbitrarily selected cases. To date, the competition project database comprises 184 projects. These too can be studied in the Internet.
(http://www.zukunftsregionen.de/projekt-boerse/main.htm)

Example 1: Derelict site rehabilitation in the 'Chemnitz/Zwickau Economic Region', Saxony

Run by: Chemnitzer Land District Administrator's Office

The 'Chemnitz/Zwickau Economic Region' in Saxony is, like most of central and eastern Europe, characterized by extreme industrial decline. This structural crisis has given rise to a huge number of often contaminated derelict sites. The first step towards rehabilitating these areas involves drawing up a new regional derelict-site register containing spatial information about buildings and premises, the current need for clarification and action as well as recommendations regarding specific forms of action.

Selected projects involve demonstrating the degree to which sustainability and the unity of ecological, economical and social demands are enabled. The aim is:

1. to identify derelict industrial and commercial sites in the region as a whole and to produce a comparative assessment as well as laying down priorities. The register is required to spell out legal and organizational handicaps and is to contain proposals for solutions

2. to create new strategies for the reuse and promotion of derelict sites

3. to re-integrate disused properties or transport infrastructure into the economic system

4. to scale down new building on open land

5. to protect areas against further pollution

6. to create jobs during the process of revitalization

Figure 1 "Regions of the Future"

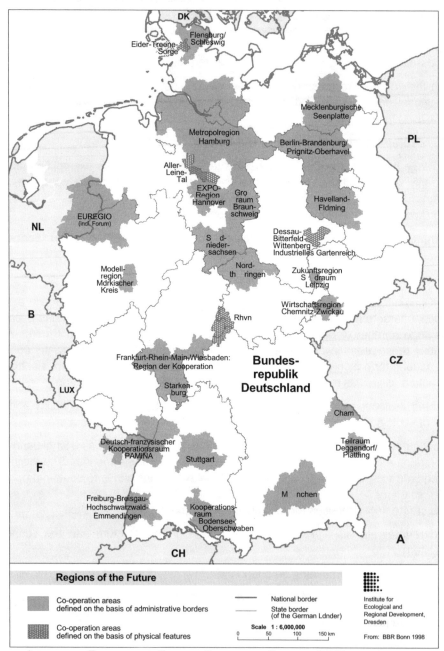

Source: INSTITUTE FOR ECOLOGICAL AND REGIONAL DEVELOPMENT DRESDEN, 1998

Example 2: 'HafenCity Hamburg' (Hamburg Docklands)

Run by: City of Hamburg

The City of Hamburg is drawing up a 'HafenCity' master plan for areas of the docks situated close to the city center (including a 390-acre stretch of water). The restructuring of this area would generate space for an extension of the inner city by means of a metropolitan mix of residential, commercial, cultural and entertainment sites. The attractive location by the river Elbe provides an opportunity to develop a lively, distinctive maritime quarter with feed-on effects for the entire city and metropolitan region. As a first step in a cooperative development process, an international 'HafenCity Hamburg' urban development competition was launched this year.

Example 3: 'Schleswig-Holsteins Haushalte machen mit!' (Households in Schleswig-Holstein join in!)

Run by: City of Elmshorn, Schleswig-Holstein Ministry for Environment, Nature and Forestry

By supporting and developing a sustainable consumer attitude, the project is focusing on implementing an existing 'Local Agenda 21' scheme in Elmshorn. For 6 months, private households are testing the extent to which it is possible to live day-to-day life in a sustainable, i.e. economically, socially and environmentally sound way. The following areas of action have been covered: waste, mobility, nutrition, energy, water and clothing. The crucial point for the initiators of the project is not to dictate how participants should act but to make households become aware of their patterns of behaviour. They themselves decide what they want to change in their everyday lives and they set their own targets. It is not a question of being perfect: one ought to be allowed to find one's own way to sustainability.

2.8 European reference regions in the German competition

Within the framework of the "Regions of the Future" competition launched in 1997, 26 selected "Regions of the Future" in Germany are in the process of completing innovative projects for sustainable development. In order to interweave experience gained in the German competition with international insights on regional development, the German "Regions of the Future" need to enter into dialogue with regions from other European countries (ICLEI 1999).

To this end, a selection process for European Reference Regions to complement the German "Regions of the Future" competition was sponsored by the Federal Office for Building and Regional Planning (BBR) and the German Association of Town, Regional and State Planning (SRL). This process was coordinated by the European Secretariat of the International Council for Local Environmental Initiatives (ICLEI)[2].

In direct correspondence with the 26 German "Regions of the Future", the 26 European Reference Regions were selected in the spring of 1999 (Table 1, Figure 2).

---

[2] For further details on the European Reference Regions see http://www.iclei.org/europe/regions/

The selection was conducted more or less using the same four principal criteria as in Germany, with additional attention given to

... the representation of regions throughout Europe

... the variety of types of regional settlement patterns.

As with the German regions, the European Reference Regions will have the opportunity to present their activities at the URBAN 21 Global Conference in Berlin. Before that conference, the 3rd Biennial of Towns and Town Planners in Europe ("3. Europäische Planerbiennale"), devoted to "Sustainable Development – A Challenge for Europe's Urban Regions", will have taken place from September 14 – 19, 1999 at Herne in the Ruhr in Germany. The 3rd Biennial offers a platform for presenting, developing and exchanging new ideas among the regions of Europe. It will work towards further specification of European and national conditions for sustainable development. 32 European regions are invited to discuss their specific problems and projects and to compare their solutions.

Table 1   The 26 European Reference Regions

- Régio Metropolitana Barcelona, Spain*
- Greater Bergen Region, Norway
- Brasov Region, Romania
- Budapest Agglomeration, Hungary*
- The Cairngorms, United Kingdom - Scotland
- Cesis Region, Latvia
- County of Dalarna, Sweden
- Dublin Region, Ireland
- Samenwerkingsverband Regio Eindhoven, Netherlands
- Emilia-Romagna, Italy*
- Erlach - östliches Seeland, Switzerland*
- Kleinregion Feldbach, Austria
- Green Dynamic Region, Denmark*
- Liguria, Italy*
- Region Midi-Pyrenees, France
- District de l'Agglomeration Nantaise, France*
- Region Nord-Pas de Calais, France*
- North West England, United Kingdom*
- Samara Agglomeration, Russia*
- Stockholm County, Sweden
- St. Petersburg Region, Russia
- Thames Valley, United Kingdom
- Transcarpathia, Ukraine
- Västernorrland, Sweden
- West of England, United Kingdom
- Zuidvleugel Region, Netherlands*

  * represented at the conference, in the exhibition and the catalogue of the 3rd Biennial at Herne in the Ruhr, September 14 – 19, 1999

Figure 2   European reference regions

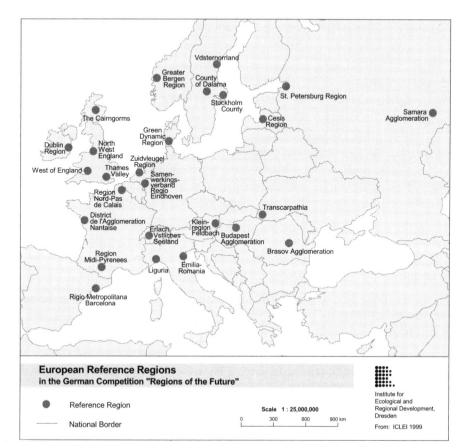

Source: INSTITUTE FOR ECOLOGICAL AND REGIONAL DEVELOPMENT DRESDEN, 1998

3.   Concluding remarks

Together with a gearing towards processes, projects and implementation, cooperations being accorded ever greater importance within regional planning in Germany. But does this necessarily mean regional planning itself is gaining in importance?

In the field of regional planning, the federal "Regions of the Future" competition is treading new ground. It is aiming to set regional sustainable development in motion by, on the one hand, creating a competitive situation between the regions and, on the other, broadening dialogue between them. In the pursuit of these aims, the competition is echoing two current trends:

Firstly, it is seeking to use "cooperative competition" as a catalyst for innovative, wide-ranging development. Comparable concepts have been in evidence in other political fields in Germany over the past decade, typical examples being the 'BioRegio' and 'InnoRegio' competitions sponsored by the Federal Ministry for Research and Education:

- 'BioRegio' addressed itself to regional networks of enterprises, research institutes and public institutions in the field of biotechnology. The three successful regions had privileged access to public research funds totalling DEM 150 million (~ 75 million €).

- 'InnoRegio' is an initiative with a similar approach currently on-going in the new federal states in eastern Germany. Regional networks are designed to enhance innovative developments of all kinds. Aims of the competition are the strengthening of regional competitiveness and the creation of jobs. For a period of 5 years, DEM 500 million (~ 250 million €) is being provided for 25 selected 'InnoRegions'.

In all cases the principal idea is the same, namely the interlinking of competition and cooperation in such a way as to develop unexploited regional potential. At the same time, the poor situation of public budgets is to be taken into account. Competitions are not geared towards blanket sponsorship but operate selectively.

But is it not the case that exchanges of experience contradict the notion of competition? Are there not conflicts between the need to cooperate interregionally and the goal of participants to outstrip their counterparts?

So far, no serious conflict is discernible between the 26 competition participants, and the competition concept does feature mechanisms that should prevent any such conflict from arising: the request to all participants to cooperate with each other, for instance, or constant urging of regional players to participate actively (ADAM 1999: 13).

Concerning the competition's planning-instrument credentials, a further observation would seem to be in order, to wit that it does not exclusively aim to promote participating regions. Rather, the concept lays claim to forming part of an all-embracing approach. It will yield promising examples of sustainable spatial and settlement development. Energetic public relations work can help disseminate the experience and knowledge acquired about sustainable regional development to many other regions all over the world.

The second trend drawn upon by the "Regions of the Future" initiative is the dialogue-driven "bottom-up approach". Communication processes are of pivotal importance in this competition. In this respect, it reflects a new understanding of planning. Given the diminishing ability of the State to regulate with the aid of statutes and rules and given also the evident lack of acceptance of 'government writ large', planning has to become more communicative. Today, coordination and convenorship are central tasks in open planning processes. This is not a trend confined to Germany. One encounters the same aspirations in, for instance, the 'Vademecum' to which the European Commission has recourse when drawing up Regional Operational Programmes for the Structural Funds or Community Initiatives.

Such processes of communication and dialogue are particularly vital to comprehensive and sustainable development. The competition looks into the regional entity as an area of cooperation, positing that "win-win strategies" are set to replace "parish-pump politics". Simultaneously, the regional scope for action increases.

It is too early to come to a final conclusion on new forms of regional cooperation for sustainable development. Though there continue to be more questions than answers, experiments such as the German "Regions of the Future" competition look very promising. The final presentation of findings, which will take place next year at the URBAN 21 Global Conference in Berlin, will not mark the end of endeavors in the spirit of sustainable regional development in Germany. It will have been a significant success, however, if it acts as a clarion call for regions to become more sustainable.

Bibliography

ADAM, BRIGITTE (1998): Der Wettbewerb "Regionen der Zukunft", Regionale Agenden für eine nachhaltige Raum- und Siedlungsentwicklung. In: UVP-report 4/98, pp. 172-175.

ADAM, BRIGITTE (1999): Der Wettbewerb "Regionen der Zukunft", Konzeption, Teilnehmer, Ablauf. In: ADAM, BRIGITTE / WIECHMANN, THORSTEN (EDS.): Neue Formen regionaler Kooperation für eine nachhaltige Entwicklung, IÖR-Text No. 121, pp. 5-17.

ADAM, BRIGITTE; BLACH, ANTONIA (1997): Strategieempfehlungen für ein raumordnerisches Modellvorhaben "Regionen der Zukunft". In: Informationen zur Raumentwicklung, 3/97, pp. 201-216.

ADAM, BRIGITTE / WIECHMANN, THORSTEN (EDS.)(1999 A): Neue Formen regionaler Kooperation für eine nachhaltige Entwicklung, IÖR-Text No. 121, pp. 31-53.

ADAM, BRIGITTE / WIECHMANN, THORSTEN (1999 B): Die Rolle der Raumplanung in regionalen Agenda-Prozessen. In: Informationen zur Raumentwicklung, 'Region' issue (forthcoming).

BUNDESFORSCHUNGSANSTALT FÜR LANDESKUNDE UND RAUMORDNUNG (BfLR) (ED.) (1997): Regionen der Zukunft, Regionale Agenden für eine nachhaltige Raum- und Siedlungsentwicklung, Wettbewerbsunterlagen, Bonn.

BUNDESAMT FÜR BAUWESEN UND RAUMORDNUNG (BBR) (ED.) (1998): Regionen der Zukunft, Regionale Agenden für eine nachhaltige Raum- und Siedlungsentwicklung, Competition Newspaper No. 1, Bonn.

BUNDESAMT FÜR BAUWESEN UND RAUMORDNUNG (BBR) (ED.) (1999): Regionen der Zukunft, Regionale Agenden für eine nachhaltige Raum- und Siedlungsentwicklung, Competition Newspaper No. 2, Bonn.

INTERNATIONAL COUNCIL FOR LOCAL ENVIRONMENTAL INITIATIVES (ICLEI) (1999): European Reference Regions in the German "Regions of the Future" competition, website: http://www.iclei.org/europe/regions/

WETTBEWERB "REGIONEN DER ZUKUNFT". In: INFORMATIONEN aus der Forschung des BBR, No. 3, July 1998, pp. 2-3.

WIECHMANN, THORSTEN (1999): Die Rolle der Regionalplanung in regionalen Agenda-Prozessen. In: ADAM, BRIGITTE / WIECHMANN, THORSTEN (EDS.): Neue Formen regionaler Kooperation für eine nachhaltige Entwicklung, IÖR-Texte No. 121, pp. 31-53

Nordic Periphery –
Firm-oriented Incentives and Potential of Networking

Mika Rantakokko

The following article is dealing with some national business funding schemes from Finland, Scotland, Sweden and Norway, and gives some examples of R&D and seed-funding opportunities. Furthermore it shows a northern view concerning the challenges and possibilities in networking.

To be able to execute a business plan an entrepreneur invariably needs some kind of support. Besides money, entrepreneurs need support so they can develop from their surroundings in the form of services, infrastructure etc. their ideas into profitable businesses. In most cases this support is a combination of both categories, financial and otherwise.

When formulating their competitive advantages, countries and regions must be able to offer ideal combinations of support forms related to the branches they are interested in promoting. Especially in the northern parts of Europe this is a very challenging task. This means that when developing the business support infrastructure – like availability of skilled labor, R&D facilities and good connections – it is necessary to be able to compensate for the negative effects of long distances and remoteness. On the other hand, it is important to use the region's strengths as effectively as possible.

1. Aid to complement market financing

Because of market failure in financing, government intervention is sometimes justified. This is particularly relevant in the development of small companies. Another objective of business aid is to promote regional development. Here are some of the main forms of business aid country by country.

1.1 Finland

Regional policy instruments in Finland have traditionally been conceived as business development measures with some elements of training, R&D and transport. The three core regional incentives in Finland comprise:

- Regional Investment Aid
- Regional Transport Subsidy, both of which are administered by the Ministry of Trade and Industry
- Regional Tax Relief, which is administered by the Ministry of Finance.

1.1.1 Regional Investment Aid

Regional Investment Aid is a discretionary grant available to companies undertaking investment projects in the three Development Areas and 11 Structural Change Areas. The main sectoral focus is on manufacturing, tourism and business services. Eligible investment projects must meet one of the following conditions:

- improve technical standards of products or production processes
- improve productivity
- strengthen the regional production structure
- reduce unemployment

The following data shows the statistics concerning the Regional Investment Aid in Finland during the period from 1993 to 1997. Data for 1996 and 1997 relate only to Structural Fund areas for Objectives 2, 5b and 6 in Finland. However, policy has become increasingly focused on these areas so that they now account for 90 percent of expenditure.

Number of awards

Year	1993	1994	1995	1996	1997
Number of Projects	2,655	2,045	1,932	4,76	5,55

Incentive cost

Year	1993	1994	1995	1996	1997
1 FIM (million)	358.7	562.0	370.5	143.7	155.4
million €	~ 60	~ 95	~ 62	~ 24	~ 26

Investment associated

Year	1993	1994	1995	1996	1997
1 FIM (million)	2,028.2	3,195	1,634	1,081.6	1,577.9
million €	~ 341	~ 537	~ 275	~ 182	~ 265

Jobs associated

Year	1993	1994	1995	1996	1997
	1,877	3,140	3,318	2,217	2,974

1.1.2 Regional Transport Subsidy

The Regional Transport Subsidy was first introduced in 1973 to compensate for the competitive disadvantage faced by companies located in the north and east of Finland. The subsidies are provided for the transport of manufactured goods to and from the Development Areas. The scheme covers transport by road, rail and ship from the place of processing. The award rates vary between 5 percent and 27 percent depending on the Development Area and the distance covered. Since 1995, the scheme has only been available to SMEs. At the moment there are plans to terminate the use of this subsidy.

1.1.3 Regional Tax Relief

Regional Tax Relief has been a long-standing element of enterprise-oriented support operated by the Ministry of Finance. This relief takes the form of a free depreciation allowance and an exemption from stamp duty. In 1994, the scheme was revised to take the form of an increased depreciation allowance, limited to three years following the investment. It is available in Development Areas 1 and 2.

Alongside these core incentives, there are also other national aids which are generally targeted at SMEs and include investment and development loans and start-up grants. There are four of these types of incentive:

- *Finnvera Loans* comprising loans for company investment, and operating capital administered by Finnvera, a public bank

- the *Small Business Aid* scheme offering investment and start-up (job creation) grants (administered by the Ministry of Trade and Industry)

- *Development Aid* offering assistance for SMEs (also administered by the Ministry of Trade and Industry)

- *Financing for Rural Industries*, a small business aid scheme for rural industries on farms comprising investment, start-up (job creation) and development grants and investment loans administered by the Ministry of Agriculture and Forestry

Finnvera is a specialized financing company promoting Finnish exports by offering export credit guarantees and supporting domestic operations of small and medium sized companies by offering risk financing and guarantees. The company is owned entirely by the Finnish state. Finnvera works closely with financial institutions and companies to be able to complement the Finnish financial market with risk financing and export credit guarantee products.

Finnvera's domestic development and financing solutions are particularly geared towards small and medium-sized companies, and thus Finnvera also helps to promote the government's regional policy objectives. Finnvera provides Finnish enterprises with a wide range of products which cover all the stages of a company's development. Export credit guarantees provide exporting companies and financiers with coverage against commercial and/or political credit risks and enable the companies to finance export trade.

Domestic loans and securities are directed at supporting business start-ups and development, domestic supplies and investment. Most of the financing decisions relating to domestic business operations are made by one of the 15 regional offices.

Sectorial aid under special conditions

Sectoral aid schemes have been utilized to solve problems due to special conditions in the food and the shipbuilding industries. Sectoral support will be abolished as soon as possible. The adjustment of the food industry to EU membership and the common market for agricultural products require support for the transition period that was agreed upon during the membership negotiations. This aid will be granted even to big companies for projects begun in 1999.

From the year 2000, EU co-financed investment subsidies will be granted to primary food industries, mainly to SMEs, subject to the general criteria for business aid. The international shipbuilding market has suffered for years from unfair competition caused by the direct impact of State aid on the prices of vessels.

Aid for internationalization

Internationalization aid is granted with the objective of lowering the threshold for SMEs to start exporting and creating a comprehensive and diverse base of Finnish export companies. Particular support targets during the report year were the internationalization of SMEs, other intangible development, and networking. The aid was focused on environmental technology, welfare, building construction and food industry clusters, as well as on service industries.

Justified plans for the use of internationalization aid were submitted by 1,200 enterprises. Aid was granted to nearly 1,000 applicants. Aid for companies was decided by the TE Centers. The Ministry decided on company-specific project aid and aid for projects to be implemented by line of business on the national scale. Most of the aid was granted to the metal and engineering industry (44%), the service industry (23%), and the food industry (15%).

The *maximum rates* of all the awards vary according to the location of the project; the highest rate of 35 percent is available in Development Area 1. SMEs may receive up to 10 percentage points more than the basic maximum, albeit within with an overall ceiling of 37 percent. All maximum rates can be exceeded by up to 5 percent when regional assistance is cumulated with other non-regional assistance.

A new Act on the general conditions for business aid came into force at the beginning of 1998. This Act directs business aid mainly towards intangible development and the promotion of the long-term competitiveness of SMEs. Large companies can receive subsidies only in exceptional circumstances. The corporate aid programs must be temporary and their effectiveness should be assessed regularly.

Business aid can only be granted to companies with ongoing profitability prospects. The profitability of the project, the total financing, and the impact on competition, such as effects on market shares and capacity, must be assessed in the decision to grant support.

Investment support, development subsidies for SMEs and operating conditions subsidies have boosted start-ups of new companies, strengthened competitiveness, and improved the business environment. Most of the business aid was granted as national co-financing in connection with financing from the European Regional Development Fund (ERDF).

1.2   Scotland

The Scottish example concerns Highlands & Islands. Highlands & Islands Enterprise (HIE) is a government sponsored development agency which sets the strategic background in which its Local Enterprise Companies operate. Local Enterprise Companies (LECs) are then contracted to HIE to deliver its programs and pursue development in a way that matches local needs. In the case of HIE there are 10 LECs in the region. This network uses various financial support incentives to enhance new businesses.

Finance for Business Development has four main forms:
- Development Grant
- Building Grant
- Interest Relief Grant
- Loan

The normal maximum level of assistance is 50% of the development costs, but the final level of assistance approved will depend on the needs of the particular case.

Development costs which are eligible for assistance include building costs, plant and equipment (new or second hand), working capital, and training programmes (considered separately below). The forms of assistance can be summarized as follows:

1.2.1 Development Grant

A Development Grant can be applied towards the purchase of a plant and equipment (new or second hand) and with working capital requirements. The normal level of this grant is 20%.

1.2.2 Building Grant

A Building Grant can be provided towards the costs of constructing new buildings or adapting, improving or extending existing buildings. The maximum rate of this grant is 35%.

1.2.3 Interest Relief Grant (IRG)

An Interest Relief Grant can be employed where the developer can secure commercial borrowing from other sources, yet requires assistance with the interest costs. The amount of this grant is derived from a notional loan and there are two rates of payment. An IRG is available for various periods, but a period of four years is normal.

1.2.4 Loan

The period, repayment pattern and interest rates of a Development Loan will be arranged to suit the particular requirements of the individual proposal. Loans are generally offered at concessionary interest rates. The interest rates are fixed for the duration of the loan and are charged on the outstanding balance of capital. Under certain circumstances, it is also possible to arrange for loans to have an interest free period and capital repayment deferment at the start of the loan; exceptionally, periods of up to 3 years are considered. Normally loans may be for periods of up to 10 years but may be up to 20 years for loans on buildings.

1.3   Sweden

Swedish regional policy offers a wide range of assistance for projects and activities in a number of designated areas. This range stretches from financial measures such as grants and loans to advisory business support measures or the establishment of industrial development centers. The financial measures consist of four grants, a loan and a concession on social security contributions. The grants are:

- Regional Development Grant for Hard Investment
- Regional Development Grant for Soft Investment (previously called the Location Grant and the Development Grant respectively)
- Employment Grant
- Transport Grant

1.3.1 Regional Development Grant

The Regional Development Grant for Hard Investment is a discretionary, project-related capital grant allowing enterprises up to 35 percent of eligible investment in Area 1 and 20 percent in Area 2 and certain temporarily-designated municipalities. SMEs are eligible for up to 40 percent of their investment costs in Aid Area 1. The combination of Regional Development Grant for Hard Investment and other State aid cannot exceed 70 percent of eligible investment in Area 1 or 50 percent in Area 2 and the temporary areas.

The award of a Regional Development Grant for Hard Investment is contingent on job and other targets being fulfilled. If agreed targets are not met, the grant can be "reclaimed" by the authorities. Such powers of reclaim diminish over time. Thirty percent becomes "non-reclaimable" at the end of the first year after payment and a further 25 percent at the end of year two. At the end of each of the succeeding three years, 20, 15 and 10 percent of the grant is similarly treated so that the entire grant is "non-reclaimable" after five years.

1.3.2 The Regional Development Grant for Soft Investment

The Regional Development Grant for Soft Investment provides support for intangible investments (product development, marketing, education etc.) in all assisted areas. This grant is worth up to 35 percent of eligible investment in Aid Area 1 and up to 20 percent in Aid Area 2 and the temporary areas. SMEs are, again, eligible for up to 40 percent of their investment costs in Aid Area 1.

1.3.3 The Employment Grant

The Employment Grant, an incentive type rare in Europe, takes the form of a fixed sum paid annually for up to five years according to additional labor taken on by firms located in Aid Areas 1 and 2. The rate of award and its duration are determined by the location of the firm, with Employment Grants payable in Areas 1 and 2 at maximum levels of SEK 200,000 (~ 23,385 €) and SEK 120,000 (~ 14,000 €) respectively over a period of five years.

1.3.4 Transport Grant

The Transport Grant is an automatic grant whose purpose is to assist manufacturing companies, in specific sectors, to transport their products to distant markets and to deliver raw materials to outlying regions. The subsidy is paid to companies that have their operations in northern Sweden (Norrland and large areas of Värmland and Dalarna) with the exception of primary industries. To be eligible, a firm's transport costs must exceed SEK 25,000 (~ 2,925 €) per annum. The grants vary between 5 and 45 percent of net expenditure, depending on the location and distance. Transport subsidies are administered by NUTEK (Swedish National Board for Industrial and Technical Development).

Two further measures are worth mentioning, The Location Loan and the Social Security Concession. The Location Loan was an important element of the Swedish Regional Incentive package in the 1980s but was withdrawn in 1990. It was then re-introduced in 1992, albeit on close to commercial terms. Its purpose is to assist companies in the Swedish assisted areas that experience difficulty in obtaining loans from commercial sources. NUTEK administers the loan, but the County Administration Boards take decisions on loan applications for amounts of up to SEK 20 million (2.34 million €).

The Social Security Concession comprises an automatic reduction on social security tax contributions paid by employers within designated areas (which coincide largely with the regional policy assisted areas). First introduced in 1983 on a pilot basis in the northernmost parts of Sweden, its current terminal date is the end of the year 2000. Available to a wide range of sectors, the objective of the concession is to make it easier for companies to both maintain current levels of staffing and to employ additional staff.

Rates of Award – Maximum rates of award vary by area and, as a percentage of eligible expenditure, are as follows:

Eligible Areas	Grant Percentage [1]
1	35[2]
2	20
Temporary Areas	20

(1) Grants to local authorities and private firms to build factories for letting and to prepare ground for peat production are set at five percentage points below these maxima

(2) Small and medium-sized enterprises (SMEs) are eligible for grants up to 40 percent of their investment costs in Aid Area 1

Award Statistics

The statistics below include awards made under regional development grants for hard and soft investment. Although these figures include awards for the location and conditional loans, these will be phased out in January 1, 1999. The source for the statistics below is NUTEK.

Number of awards

Year	1992/93	1993/94	1994/95	1995/96	1996/97
1 Number approved	538	769	665	537	291

Incentive cost (in million)

Year	1992/93	1993/94	1994/95	1995/96	1996/97
Awards approved (SEK)	430	645	805	873	519
Awards approved (€)	~ 50	~ 75	~ 95	~ 102	~ 60

Investment associated (in million)

Year	1992/93	1993/94	1994/95	1995/96	1996/97
Eligible investment (SEK)	1,544	2,573	3028.4	3,069.9	2625
Eligible investment (€)	~ 180	~ 300	~ 354	~ 359	~ 306

Jobs associated

Year	1992/93	1993/94	1994/95	1995/96	1996/97
Employment associated*	2,473	3,865	3,883	3,763	2,935

Based on applicant estimates of jobs associated

1.4 Norway

The Norwegian Industrial and Regional Development Fund was established by a special Act, pursuant to the Act relating to State-owned Enterprises. The fund was established to increase the efficiency of the total system of industry-directed instruments, and to simplify procedures for potential users in business and industry. The fund, which is entirely owned by the State, is administratively subordinate to the Ministry of Industry and Energy. Its headquarters are in Oslo, and it has five regional offices, respectively, in Bergen, Bodø, Kristiansand, Trondheim and Ålesund. In addition, the business and industry departments in the county municipalities provide guidance on the fund's countrywide measures, and deal with cases for the fund's measures directed towards rural districts.

Most of the fund's activities are associated with loans, guarantees and grants. There are several schemes for loans, guarantees and grants, some of which apply everywhere in the country whereas others are directed specifically towards businesses in sparsely populated areas. The loans are given either as secured loans for medium and long-term investments in building and machinery or as risk capital loans for investment, company establishments, restructuring and development projects. In 1995, the fund had a total budget of NOK 2,666 million (~ 320,000 €) for loans and guarantees, and of NOK 1,485 million (~ 178,000 €) for grants.

The fund also has an equity scheme that can be used to invest in shares in small and medium-sized companies. This is done to strengthen the equity base in business and industry. In 1995 NOK 400 million (~ 48.04 million €) had been set aside for the equity scheme.

The fund also runs several programs of different kinds:

- The network program is intended to stimulate small companies to cooperate with other companies and research institutions

- Plan of action for the tourist trade where the objective is to increase productivity, competitiveness and profitability in the tourist trade

- FRAM, which aims at improving the profitability of small companies by means of strategy and management development

The fund carries out management assignments for the State, such as the Venture Fund, environmental impact assessments regulated in the Planning and Building Act, as well as functioning as the secretariat for the Government Bank Investment Fund and the State Newspaper Loan Fund.

2. Focus on R&D

Every country has its own systems to finance R&D. For example in Finland this responsibility is assumed by Tekes, the National Technology Agency. It is the main financing organization for applied and industrial R&D in Finland. The funds for financing are awarded from the state budget. Tekes also offers channels for cooperation with Finnish companies, universities and research institutes. It coordinates and offers financial support for participation in international technology initiatives, including EU research programs, EUREKA, research activities of OECD's energy organization IEA (International Energy Agency), European Cooperation in Scientific and Technical research (COST), European Space Agency (ESA) and Nordic cooperation.

Tekes also offers a network of Scientific Counselors and Attachés whose aim is to increase technological cooperation between their base countries and Finland.

Tekes uses technology programs to promote development in specific sectors of technology or industry, and to pass on results of the research work to business in an efficient way. These programs have proved to be an effective form of cooperation and networking for companies and the research sector.

During 1999, a total of over 60 extensive national technology programs are under way. Program themes cover the whole variety of Finnish special branches stretching from nanotechnology and electronics to the furniture industry. In 1998, Tekes provided FIM 885 million (~ 149 million €) to financing technology programs.

Technology programs are planned in cooperation with companies, research institutes, and Tekes. The planning takes place in working groups and open preparatory seminars. The duration of the programs ranges from three to five years; their volumes range from FIM 30 million (~ 5 million €) to hundreds of millions of Finnish marks. Tekes usually finances about half of the costs of such programs. The second half comes from participating companies.

The main benefits lay in the close cooperation between research institutes and industry, the widespread involvement of small and medium sized companies, and the high level of international cooperation.

2.1 Nordic R&D financier

The Nordic Industrial Fund is the collaborative body for the Nordic countries in industrial research and development (R&D). Its job is to stimulate, initiate and finance R&D in Nordic industry. By doing that they promote innovation, strengthen competitiveness and encourage internationalization. They do that in conjunction with the national R&D financing institutions. The most important target group is dynamic small and medium sized enterprises. The Nordic Industrial Fund is an official institution under the administration of the Nordic Council of Ministers.

NIF supports industrially oriented R&D projects where at least two Nordic countries are involved. They can finance up to 50 per cent of the project's total budget. The companies involved are responsible for the remaining half. NIF concentrates on smaller R&D projects lasting not longer than three years, the contribution does normally not exceed NOK 5 million (~ 0.6 million €).

3. Examples of seed financing programs

There are also various forms of seed financing programs, which can be even region-specific. Here two examples:

3.1 Some seed financing possibilities in Oulu region

OuluTech Ltd., which is a company owned by the University of Oulu, Sitra (Finnish National Fund for Research and Development) and Technopolis Oulu Plc., commercializes technology-based ideas, inventions and research results in Finland and abroad, including the obtaining of patents, further product development and marketing. They also help to start up enterprises based on research and product development projects, and to transfer innovations to be utilized by the enterprises already established.

OuluTech also plays a role in seed financing. Via OuluTech the region of Oulu has its own seed financing program. The municipalities in the region finance the program. This fund aims to support manufacturing and service-oriented start-up companies with some growth potential. Maximum investment is FIM 500,000 (~ 85,000 €)/company (average investment FIM 250,000 (~ 42,500 €). The fund makes 3 – 5 investments per year. Payback happens by royalty, which varies between 2 to 6 % of turnover during 5 (max. 7) years.

OuluTech is also in the position to offer incubator subsidies. This takes the form of a small business subsidy from the Ministry of Trade and Industry which is targeted at technology-based companies in the Oulu region. Such subsidies can vary from between FIM 100,000 an 150,000 (~ 16,800 and ~ 25,220 €) per company. The Ministry's contribution is 35 % of the total costs. The entrepreneur is obliged to sign an incubator contract with OuluTech. Clients are normally first time entrepreneurs who are starting from scratch. They may have a technical background, and little or no experience in business. The company pays a fee, which is FIM 8,000 (~ 1,350 €) per year plus 0.5 % of the turnover. Contracts are for five years.

3.2 Highland Prospect Ltd.

The objective of the company is to support local and inward investment opportunities. Highland Prospect Limited was established to respond to approaches from the private sector to participate in securing major investment projects in the Highlands of Scotland.

The resources of the company are available to support local and inward investment opportunities, and are to be considered complementary to sources of public and private sector assistance.

The company is particularly conscious of the high threshold costs associated with expanding or establishing any new venture especially in the initial years of operation. The intention is to therefore focus on those areas of private sector investment which would not take place without the company's participation.

These provisions will remain constantly under review by the company to exploit new and expanding economic development activities.

Assistance is available from the company as discretionary finance to encourage major economic investment in the Highlands. Inquiries for assistance are open to all those who are, or propose to be, involved in establishing or developing a major business enterprise in the Highlands.

The type of financial assistance can generally be split into the following categories:

- Property development undertaken by the company for and on behalf of an identified occupant/occupier
- Low interest secured loans

The type of projects that can be assisted are generally in the following three areas of activity:

- Manufacturing/Processing Industry
- Service Sector
- Tourism/Leisure-related

The company does not wish to limit their level of possible investment in any one project, however, in general terms it is highly unlikely that any investment will be offered above 50% of the total project costs.

Highland Prospect will attempt to ensure that appropriate packages of assistance, including that from the company and other possible sources are identified. Sources of matching funds should be approached at the same time as Highland Prospect Limited to avoid possible delays in the time it takes for an application to be processed.

4. It is not only the money

Northern Europe is a very sparsely populated region. For example in the Nordic countries there are a total of 24 million inhabitants (equal to the total population of the Benelux countries) living on an area measuring 1.2 million km^2 (approximately the size of Germany, France, Great Britain and the Benelux countries). Population density in the northernmost parts of this region is even more sparse. For example in Finnish Lapland there are 7 municipalities with less than one inhabitant per square km. These seven municipalities, which have a land area of 57,000 km^2, are home to 30,000 people – the population of a small town living in an area almost equal to Ireland! The special character of this region was recognized for example when the European Union developed a new priority objective – Objective 6 (regions with extremely low population density) for the northernmost parts of Finland and Sweden.

The special circumstances found in the northernmost parts of Europe pose special challenges. Yet all their natural resources have provided the basis for many industries. In many branches there is also very high level of expertise. On the other hand long distances and the relatively remote location have required major investments in the public infrastructure, including public services and transportation networks.

How to maximize the strengths of the region while minimizing the effect of negative factors? How to find a niche in the international markets, where the role of old-fashioned competitive advantages doesn't exist any longer? Development of new innovations/innovative processes plays a very central role.

In the following section there are some examples of how innovation support can be handled at different regional levels in the northernmost part of Europe. The common denominator in all of these examples is cooperation, in its different forms.

4.1 Northern Periphery program

Northern Periphery is an ERDF Article 10-funded program in the field of Transnational Regional Planning, promoting cooperation between the northernmost parts of Finland, Scotland, Sweden and Norway. The program's background is described in the European Spatial Development Perspective document.

There are 2.3 million people living in the program region, which has an area of 615, 000 km^2. This region can be characterized by the term regional fragmentation; there are centers which are separated by vast areas with very tiny settlements. In all four countries the target areas are quite some distance from major centers. Enterprises in the region are suffering from small home markets and are experiencing difficulty in breaking into much larger export markets.

The overall objective for the program is to contribute to the improvement of services and value creation in the Northern Periphery in ways compatible with the principles of sustainable development, through transnational exchange of experiences. This will involve cooperation in the field of spatial planning as it affects the development of business activities and social services in the target area. Cooperation will not involve planning processes for a common transnational region, but will focus on the exchange of good practice for spatial planning within each participating region.

The joint strategy for this program is focused on the development of new knowledge about innovative and effective solutions for sustainable business activity, service provision and land use/local spatial development planning in northern peripheral areas characterized by extremely sparse population, long distances and harsh climate.

The program's total budget is 13.33 million €. The program is implemented through sub-actions of:

(1) Pilot projects involving the provision of services (4 million €)

(2) Pilot projects concerning business development and sustainable resource management (5.33 million €)

(3) Documentation and exchange of good practice (3.33 million €)

In an innovation and business support context the Northern Periphery program can support experiments that aim at finding successful ways to exploit the regional business opportunities, documentation of examples of good practice and exchange of experiences.

Under the first two sub-actions there are several relevant project themes which are directly related to innovation and business support:

- Use of information technology to provide specialized business services and market information
- Provision of advice and information on locational questions for new businesses
- Joint marketing strategies
- Commercial activities based on Northern/Arctic conditions
- Establishing functional linkages between SMEs and their most important partners
- Increasing interaction and mobility among universities/high-schools, local companies and local development organizations
- Establishing export and marketing cooperation among SMEs
- Cooperative production in networks of small scale manufacturers

The program started its activities March 1998 and the first deadline for applicants was April 3, 1998. One example of project which is related to innovation support and which has good chances of being financed in the first round is the project in telemedicine, where five northern know-how centers work together, specializing on their own expertise and yet collecting their experiences into one whole. This project could result some new commercial products. Another example is the project arranging possibilities for enterprises to meet each other; at the moment there isn't too much transnational information and linkages between enterprises working in these northern regions – despite the fact that they are working on same branches.

4.2 RIS Northern EU

One way of facing the lack of understanding when it comes to innovative processes is to develop regional innovation strategies. The European Commission has been playing a very active role in this field by supporting financially the preparation of such strategies among other things.

In this connection Oulu Technopolis Ltd., Finland, and the Aurorum Science Park in Luleå, Sweden, are implementing a project called "RIS Northern EU". The aim of the RIS (Regional Innovation Strategies) Northern EU project, which focuses on expanding concrete cooperation between companies in Northern Finland and Northern Sweden, is to integrate the top-level competence available in these regions. The aim of this collaboration, in turn, is to improve the competitive capacity and technological expertise of local SMEs.

One of the most important objectives of this project, which was launched by the Oulu Region Centre of Expertise in April 1997, was to draw up a hi-tech strategy for the northernmost EU area and to increase entrepreneurs' knowledge of each other in regional terms.

The projects' central branches are:
- electronics
- software technology
- space technology
- metal industry
- pulp and paper industry
- environmental technology

Branches were selected to cover the most essential fields in terms of innovation; All of these fields are located in both Norrbotten, Sweden and in the three northernmost regions of Finland.

The project's working methods are very pragmatic, trying to create new cross-border linkages between northern Finland and northern Sweden. This "marrying" happens at every possible level, starting from individual enterprises and ending up with regional authorities which are responsible for supporting new innovations and creating the optimal preconditions for the birth of new innovations.

There have already been some encouraging results; there are already several new collaboration projects aiming at new innovations in the fields of environmental technology, measurement technology, cold conditions know-how, multimedia and telemedicine. A platform to develop a common vision of the innovation support in this northern region together with entrepreneurs has been offered to regional development authorities. This strategy is in the process of being formulated.

4.3 TRIPS Northern EU – developing a virtual cluster

It has been noticed that entrepreneurs on either side of the border do not know anything about each other, in spite of being active in the same branches. To improve this situation the next step in the RIS project has been developed, called TRIPS Northern EU. The focus will be on the creation of common innovation support infrastructure.

By using the latest telecommunication tools a virtual cluster of hi-tech expertise will be developed. The virtual character for the cluster is essential because the individual actors in this network can in reality be almost one thousand kilometers from each other!

The network will offer possibilities not only to cooperate in terms of product development and production, but also for things like international marketing and technology surveillance. This cooperation can play a very central role when new and small enterprises with a weak economical basis but with very strong innovative potential are concerned.

4.4 Multipolis-Network

A new network, called "Multipolis", will comprise independent hi-tech centers in more than 10 locations in Northern Finland. These centers which will share a joint business strategy that defines the sector of expertise of each on the basis of market needs. The project also involves the University of Oulu and other institutions of higher education.

A survey has been started which will also act as an aid to developing the EU program for the next period in a manner which will take into consideration the needs of hi-tech companies.

To minimize the effect of such huge distances the independent hi-tech centers and other relevant knot-points will be closely linked together into a very fast telecommunication network. This ensures the availability of services and "the critical mass". This could mean for example that centers can each create their own special support services and spread these out to the whole Polis-network. It is also important to mention that all the polises are enterprises. This guarantees the best possible contact to service-users and flexible reactions to the market's needs.

The main idea behind the Polis-network is to create concentrations where people can work, either in the "old-fashioned way" or using different data networks and doing teleworking, making it possible for employees to live outside the center. On the other hand the effective network makes it economically possible for entrepreneurs to locate their activities also in the not-so-central areas. When technology develops further and wireless data transfer becomes even faster, the networks can be expanded to cover even larger areas, when the building of telecommunication infrastructure no longer requires wiring the regions involved.

There can be several ways of using the network, not only for innovation support, but also for specific purposes. This can be for example an effective platform networking employees and employers and working on developing new solutions for service provision and education.

Politically the Multipolis-model can combine different interests. Both supporters of centralization policy and decentralization policy can get their views heard; centers will be developed but in a decentralize way. In practice this model shows how to promote effectively activities requiring hi-tech by creating new infrastructure. As a proof of its functionality also enterprises have started to carry out the same model by setting up new units in different locations.

When comparing different ways of using public funding for infrastructure, the Multipolis-model offers an interesting point of view to the alternative infrastructure investments. Would it be reasonable to invest in the data networks instead of new bridges? For example over 2,000 persons have moved each year to Oulu from the sparsely populated northern regions. This development has resulted in enormous extra costs to provide housing for these people. The question is whether investing half of this sum in telecommunications would slow down this migration.

4.5 Ii Micropolis

Successful cooperation between the Oulu Region and the Ii Local Council in 1997 led to the establishment of the science park known as Micropolis at Ii, some 50 km north of Oulu and in the EU Objective 6 area.

As part of the Multipolis-network, Micropolis Ltd. concentrates on the micro-electronic industry and semi-conductor technology applications. Micropolis is a technological working environment for the micro-electronic industry, offering state of the art laboratory and production facilities for semi-conductor technology applications. It is situated in Northern Finland, 20 minutes drive from Oulu, enabling networking and joint ventures with many technological enterprises from Technopolis Oulu. Close mutual relations with the Technopolis Oulu Region offers flexible cooperation with the Technical Research Centre of Finland (VTT) and Oulu University. The significance of cooperation between universities and enterprises is increasing in research and product development.

The Micropolis concept is planning to be a significant semi-conductor technological conglomeration in Europe. The aim is to attain worldwide recognition. Data highway and optical fiber cable enable fast contact between customers and business associates.

Micropolis is an integrated part of the Technopolis Oulu Region and it became part of the Technopolis Oulu network when it was founded in 1997. The capability of integrating services is a key factor for the competitiveness of industrial production. Growth increasingly depends on demand-based innovation. Through joint ventures with other technological enterprises opportunities are also opening with international research institutes.

The aim of Micropolis Ltd. is to create tools and an operating environment which has such a high standard that the enterprises will grow and develop into significant manufacturers in the field of semi-conductor technology. The development operations of Micropolis Ltd. are concentrated on promoting the enterprises of the Micropolis conglomeration. Partnership with the Municipality of Ii and Technopolis Oulu gives fundamental strength to Micropolis operations. A comprehensive approach to local development entails clear understanding of the important role played by the local community. It must be involved in the partnership. This is a proof positive that globalization of the economy does not mean elimination of the local dimension.

Micropolis Ltd. is a development company. The promotion and development work is set to coherent priorities and projects.

5.   Final statement

It is important that enterprises can find financial support when they need it. On the other hand regions should be able to improve their performance as attractive locations for setting up businesses. When for example an enterprise is seeking its way into new location, it is not only money that counts; an enterprise pays attention to all factors, like availability of skilled labor and R&D facilities.

When talking about relative competitive advantages and value-added creation in the northern regions of Europe, the regional competitiveness is based on high-level expertise in some technology-based branches, like electronics and telecommunication.

Another competition factor is nature, among other things as a tourism attraction or raw material base. In this context it is notable that there are also branches which some might regard as a bit old-fashioned, but which are very innovative in their approach to nature. A good example of this is paper production which at its best uses very sophisticated methods and techniques.

Because the northern regions of Europe have a sparse community structure also the industries face special challenges there. On the other hand, logistics for example isn't the problem for enterprises which can fit their yearly production into a small suitcase – or these which require no space at all – while at the same time employing dozens of people. The problems lie elsewhere.

The key factor for enterprises which want to stay on top of technological development is the availability of skilled labor. This means that regions must have high-level education and research, producing new employees but also new innovations and spin-offs. Close cooperation between enterprises and educational institutes and research institutes results in up-to-date demand-led research and labor. When this is combined with the biggest problems in the northern regions, that is to say emigration and unemployment, the solution to the problem should be found in a better fit of supply and demand.

Cooperation needs common forums where "different sides" can meet. One form of this competition could be the virtual clusters. Virtual clusters differ from normal clusters in terms of distance; members of the virtual cluster can be far from each other, whereas the normal cluster structure requires closer physical contacts. In innovation support this could mean the separate actors are very far from each other.

Because of long distances and a limited number of know-how centers, special attention must also be paid to all forms of cooperation. This could be for example in worldwide technology surveillance and marketing. To start the cooperation different actors must have information about potential partners. Innovation support in this context would mean providing business-orientated and up-to-date information services.

In shortening the distances it is imperative to use the latest technologies. This means for example high-speed information highways. Long distances could be even turned using advanced communication networks into a competitive advantage by making the networks "too good". When the technical circumstances are "too good" the networks could serve as a test bench for new innovations.

The technology used is the latest possible and networks are functioning – yet it is still possible that nothing happens. Where is the problem? We are facing the soft side problems in innovation support. This means that technology and know-how alone aren't enough. Workers also have their lives outside their jobs. That's where the other challenges lie. For a short period, work might be enough, but in the long run ... What is also needed are high-level services like schools and many other basic services as well as recreational and cultural services to allow people to prosper.

In conclusion, business support in northern Europe is a diversified field involving technology, enterprises, supporting services and development of the "softer side". In this development work, various financial possibilities, like structural funds, play and will play a very important role of course. While making it possible for all regions – not only the northernmost parts of Europe themselves – to use and improve their own strengths and competitive advantages, all of Europe will benefit and improve its position in the increasingly harsh world of international competition.

Bibliography

Yuill, D., Bachtler, J. and F. Wishlade (1999): European Regional Incentives 1999 – Directory and Review of Regional Grants and Other Aid Available for Industrial and Business Expansion and Relocation in the Member States of the European Union and Norway, Bowker Saur, London.

Internet

Finland:	http://www.vn.fi/ktm/eng/paasivu.htm
	http://www.oulutech.fi/index2.htm
Scotland:	http://www.hie.co.uk/business/
	http://www.scotent.co.uk/
Sweden:	http://naring.regeringen.se/foretagsutveckling.htm
	http://www.nutek.se/information/english/activorg_eng.html
Norway:	http://odin.dep.no/nhd/publ/naering/part3.html#3
	http://landsdelsutvalget.no/
Northern Periphery Programme:	http://www.scotnordic.com/northernperiphery/
RIS Northern EU:	http://www.otm.fi/ris/
TRIP Northern EU, Multipolis:	http://www.otm.fi/oske/oso/

Technology, Innovation, Qualification: An All-inclusive Offer for Regions – Austrian Experiences

WALTER ORTNER

1. Some general information about the Steyr Economic Region

The Steyr Economic Region is located in the southeastern part of the province of Upper Austria, about 35 kilometers from the provinical capital of Linz and about 20 kilometers south of the *Westautobahn* (which is the freeway between Vienna and Salzburg) and the west railway line, the two most important traffic arteries in Austria.

The City of Steyr and eight other communities make up the Steyr Economic Region, a small domain with some 75,000 residents. The region is presently classified as an Objective 2 Area, in the framework of the European Union Regional Support Authority.

The high unemployment which appeared during restructuring projects of the 1980s was a key indicator for its classification as an Objective Area.

Figure 1   Steyr Economic Region – The Location

2. Yesterday's status

In general, the Steyr Region has been characterized by ironworking and metalworking since the Middle Ages. During industrialization in the middle part of the 19th century, Steyr developed into one of the most important weapon producing sites in the Austro-Hungarian monarchy.

In 1920, after the end of the monarchy, a new orientation toward the vehicle manufacturing industry began, a field which still contributes substantially to the economy of the site. Steyr-Daimler-Puch AG was the dominant firm in the city and its surroundings, and this dominance lasted until the beginning of the 1980s.

By the beginning that decade, however, Steyr-Daimler-Puch AG had slipped into a pronounced business crisis which could be attributed to several causes:

- Too much time was devoted to quality production with a much too long manufacturing depth
- The potentials and possibilities for cooperation, diversification and niche marketing were recognized too late
- High wage levels within Steyr-Daimler-Puch AG also led to stubborn inflexibility on the part of the work force

The outcome of these developments in the eighties and early nineties was shown in particular by the fact that:

- Unemployment rose markedly, at times rising above 10%, which, for Austria, is a very high relative rate
- Among the population as well as at the regional political level, aphase of insecurity concerning the viability of the Steyr Economic Centre followed
- The Centre itself looked like a site in crisis, and this status was communicated to the media

3. The path leading to today – incentives toward restructuring

Finding the path toward overcoming the crisis by restructuring can not be attributed to a single factor buth rather to the joint effects of a number of factors:

- The establishing of BMW

    The settlement of BMW Motors in Steyr was important to the economic development of the region. Tight in the midst of a crisis of the then-leading firm, Steyr-Daimler-Puch AG, this settling-in was a vital positive incentive.

- The sale (at the right time) of portions of Steyr-Daimler-Puch AG

    The sale of parts of Steyr-Daimler-Puch to the German MAN Group and to the Swedish company SKF, led to the retention of important production divisions (Utility vehicles, rolling bearings) at the Steyr site. Had the sale not taken place, the divisions would no longer be present in Steyr. Moreover, outsourcing for these and other divisions was done at the same time (toolmaking, for example).

- Finding agents and promoters for the reorganization process and the change in awareness

It was relevant that also on the political, economic and scientific levels, more agents and promoters were found who saw that active reorganization and process of further development were ways to surmount the crisis.

- The conceiving and founding of FAZAT Steyr

  FAZAT Steyr assumed the central role in this reorientation process. Initially described as an "unrealizable vision", it ahs today become a visible sign of the positive future design of the entire Steyr region.

4. The situation today

4.1 At the enterprise level

With regard to enterprise structure, the Steyr site is presently characterized by two features:

1. It has become a site of internationally-active companies. The essential, relevant fact is that all of these companies not only produce in Steyr, but also make use of local research, development and engineering facilities.

2. In the fields of engineering, technical consultation and software development, the near-to-production services sector has continued to develop in recent years in terms of both quality and quantity.

This attention to services is also found within the industrial enterprises themselves, as they have expanded their own research, development and engineering departments.

Some examples:

BMW Motors	Engine production; integrated diesel engine development center
SKF Austria	Development and production of special anti-friction bearings; integrated measuring-practice center
Steyr-Daimler-Puch Technology Centre	Engineering center with emphasis on motor vehicle technology

4.2 The employment market

The developments outlined have also had a positive effect on the regional employment market. While unemployment in Austria has risen – compared to a generally low unemployment rate in other countries of the European Union, in Steyr it is declining. However, Steyr has not yet attained the favorable average employment level of Upper Austria as a whole.

4.3. Training- and technological infrastructure

The high educational level of the region, especially that of skilled workers and technicians, ranks high among the strengths of the Steyr region today. With the establishment of FAZAT Steyr, which I will now consider in greater detail, a modern infrastructure has been created over the past ten years, and with it the competence of the site has developed even further.

5. Research and Training Centre for Labour and Technology – FAZAT Steyr

5.1 The concept and setting of goals

The idea of founding FAZAT Steyr first emerged back in the year 1986. JOSEF WEIDENHOLZER, a Professor at Linz University and today Director of the Austrian Labour Marketing Service, HERBERT BUCHINGER and myself, first sketched out the principal characteristics of FAZAT Steyr. In contrast to many of the technology centers coming into existence in Austria at that time, FAZAT was conceived as an innovation-promoting infrastructure.

In the starting phase these abstract objectives made it difficult for such a medium-term-oriente project to exert a positive effect at the regional level, a situation which dogged FAZAT Steyr during its early years.

5.2 The location – the construction stages

As the site for the future Centre, a historical but desolate factory building near the city center was selected. It was renovated and adapted for its new role in three construction stages stretching over the years 1990 to 1998. This step-by-step development procedure was based not solely on financial motives, but also made it possible to allow experience obtained in the preceding step to influence the next step in construction.

FAZAT Steyr thus gained not only a politically innovative function, but also made a significant contribution to city development and more particularly to cultural awareness.

Since the construction and development of FAZAT Steyr did not take place at city limits or on a green meadow somewhere, but, right in the heart of the city, the inhabitants of Steyr saw and now see FAZAT Steyr grow and develop whereas they observed it at first with skepticism, then with interest, today they view it with pride.

Figure 2 Research and Training Center for Labour and Technology (FAZAT)

August 1989   September 1998

5.3. Organizing and financing

In 1989 FAZAT Steyr had to decide with which regional proponents it should join forces in order to form the necessary foundation for putting its plans into action.

In the course of the second construction step, as the project grew, the organization developed further. In 1992 the FAZAT Association founded, together with the City of Steyr, an operating company which took over the conceptual work and management tasks. With final completion of FAZAT Steyr in autumn of 1998, FAZAT Steyr GmbH was further enlarged to include the "Upper Austrian Technology and Marketing Association" (TMG-OÖ) and the federal "Technology Impulse Association" (TIG), a development which will be of major significance in planning for the future.

Overview of the development of FAZAT Steyr

	FAZAT I	FAZAT II	FAZAT III
Start of operation	1990	1994	1998
Usable area (m^2)	620	1,300	3,560
Construction costs (in million ATS/ €)	13.8/1.1	37.1/2.70	100.0/7.27

Financing the three construction stages (total costs 151 million ATS/10.97 million Euros) of FAZAT Steyr was made possible by the collaboration of several public institutions.

	in millions ATS	in millions €	in %
City of Steyr	50.0	3.63	33.1
Upper Austrian Provincial Government	24.5	1.78	16.2
Federal Ministries (all together) - Science and Transport - Commercial Affairs - Labor and Social Welfare	33.6	2.44	22.3
European Regional Development Fund (ERDF)	17.5	1.27	11.6
FAZAT Association	25.3	1.84	16.8
Totals	**150.9**	**10.97**	**100.0**

5.4 FAZAT Steyr – Principal fields

In mid-1990, in the course of the professional conference "*Wandel mit System – Sinn und Grenzen regionaler Technologiepolitik*", the entire FAZAT Steyr concept was presented to a broad spectrum of regional development specialists.

Building upon conversations with agents of regional companies, collaboration with university-level institutions in Linz and Vienna, and an intensive series of discussions with regional political representatives, four ranges of activity (four pillars) were derived.

From this establishing of performance for the benefit of regional authorities, as well as the (future) requirements of regional enterprises, it was deemed necessary to strive to consider these pillars not in isolation, but rather as a network, coordinated for concrete projects.

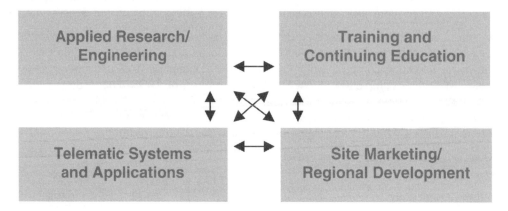

- **The principal fields (the four pillars) now in detail:**

    Applied research: The essential conformity to production-oriented research and engineering services, not only with regard to individual companies but also to networked and cooperative enterprises, is an adequate purpose in accord with the requirements of the Steyr industrial site.

- **Continuing training and education:**

    Through superior and continuing training and education competence, particularly in the production and management domains, should be further developed. Professionally-attended proposals and the planned application of computer-based training are in preparation.

- **Telematics:**

    Since they intersect other domains, telematic services and application (based increasingly on Internet technologies) have gained significance in the most varied fields of application. At the FAZAT level, this technology is vital for the other pillars: the fields of research, training and site marketing.

- **Site marketing/regional development:**

    The principal goals in the area of site marketing are to stimulate the founding of new enterprises to facilitate their settling in by offering them professional services (information, counseling, one-stop shopping), as well as to encourage the development of infrastructural offers in the form of trade zones, an industrial park and a technological center. Regional development is a continuing process. Future planning of regional site and innovation policies requires solid preparation in order for transformation to be successful.

5.5 FAZAT Steyr institutions and their performance in detail

In the development of FAZAT Steyr, FAZAT Steyr Association plays a special role. Assuming the role of a regional development agency, it was at the forefront in the conception and founding of the "Key Project" of the service area just indicated.

The goal was transformation of the "Key Project" into an independent load-carrying structure, at the same time networking this structure with the region's principal players. Today the following installations and enterprises are active in FAZAT Steyr:

Profactor Produktionsforschung GmbH	Research/Engineering and consultation in the following fields: - Quality-controlled production (solutions for problem-formulations in measurement and manufacturing technology) - Holistic engineering planning, optimization and automation of industrial processes in their entirety - Telematics-based engineering: Interdepartmental and interplant applications of modern information technology
PS Industry GmbH	Development of software solutions for industrial applications on SAP basis
KAPPA Labour Safety and Environmental Technology GmbH	Development and engineering of electronically-controlled vacuum systems
Polytechnical University of Upper Austria Steyr Campus	Curriculum: Manufacturing and Management Technology (Training, company projects, continuing education) In preparation: Course of study in International Logistics Management
Steyr Correspondence-School Centre	Studies for employed persons within the framework of courses offered by the Hagen Correspondence University (Germany)
Upper Austrian Vocational Advancement Institute Steyr Campus	Courses in electronic data processing and the Internet
Regional Information System (RIS GmbH) Shareholders: - two banks - Telekom Austria - Ennskraftwerke - Gemdat Upper Austria and the regional Telekom Association	Telematics, Internet services and applications, in the areas (among others) of: - community management - company applications (EDI, ...) - site information systems
Netzwerkstatt Kremser & Partner KEG	Founding enterprise in the areas of network, technology, Internet applications
PC Club Steyr	Experience exchange and communication platform for EDP specialists ("computer-freaks")
FAZAT Steyr GmbH	Range of activities

6. The Steyr Economic Region – tomorrow's challenges

The successful establishment of FAZAT Steyr, as well as the present "pacified" situation in the region, should not be reasons for Steyr to rest on its laurels. Instead, this status (from the viewpoints of both the installations and the principals) must be utilized as an incentive to plan further site development targets and convert those plans into action.

Action in the following areas seems to be essential:

- It would be generally effective to keep developing the knowledge base of the area. That is a precondition for highly-developed sites, in order to maintain their competitive advantages and their site quality.

  The goal, therefore, is expansion of research, training and telematic resources in both quality and quantity and strengthening their network ties.

- Cooperative activities and networks must be initiated, promoted and further developed on various levels.

  This involves increased stimulation of cooperation between enterprises, and should be coordinated with the Technology and Marketing agencies of the Province of Upper Austria.

  This is also valid for cooperation between enterprises and research, developed in particular by Profactor (see above).

- In this connection, a special role would be played by cooperation between the communities of the region with regard to site development/site marketing.

7. Site marketing in the Steyr Economic Region

The basis for the City's collaboration with the surrounding communities was created with the recognition of the Steyr Region as an Objective 2 area (1995 – 1999). For the first time in the more recent history of the region, regional interests were placed in the foreground.

In the framework of this program, the communities decided to award a "Concept for Mutual Site Marketing" contract to FAZAT Steyr Association. In the course of developing their concept, which was at the same time a procedure development, the communities also decided to join forces in a working alliance with an initial duration of two years.

The objectives of this collaboration is:

- Determining and agreeing upon a price and a promotion policy, as well as the information processes with regard to settling-in and relocation of new businesses

- The setup of a common site information system (http://www.fazat-steyr.at/sis) and a common PR strategy

- Following through with mutual advertising activities in cooperation with TMG OÖ and the Austrian Business Agency

- Improvement of regional opportunities by the development of commercial zones, as well as a Steyr Industrial Park with a Technology Centre

- Realizing all the proposed tasks and assignments through the FAZAT Steyr Associaion

Demand Overflow and Sustainability – Balearic Islands

JOANA MARIA SEGUÍ PONS, MARIA ROSA MARTÍNEZ REYNÉS

1. Introduction

The Balearic Islands lie in the western Mediterranean, off the coasts of Catalonia and Valencia. The Balearics, properly speaking, are Mallorca and Menorca and the islands comprised of Eivissa and Formentera, more southerly and closer to the Valencian coast. The Balearic archipelago has other, smaller islands not permanently inhabited, among them Cabrera, now a National Park. The total area of the archipelago is 5,012 km^2. Mallorca, the largest island, has 3,640 km^2, Menorca 716 km^2, Eivissa 573 km^2 and Formentera, the smallest of the permanently inhabited islands, only 83 km^2.

Due to their strategic location, the Balearics have been visited and occupied by many cultures. In antiquity Phoenicians, Greeks, Carthaginians, Romans, Arabs and Catalans left their successive imprints on the island's landscape and culture. More recently, aristocrats, artists, painters, and writers attracted by the climate and the beauty of the landscapes have placed the Balearics in a privileged status as an internationally renowned destination.

This vocation of hospitality has evolved in the last forty years into the implantation of a model of mass tourism which, although favouring extraordinary economic expansion, has also had its costs. Imbalances in the economic structure, in social habits, in territorial dynamics and in natural habitats are the consequence of a feverish development that has seemed to ignore the limitations of the resources growth feeds upon.

In recent years, the increasing awareness of social agents and institutions, as well as the ever more urgent demand, have forced a reconsideration of the regional economy from the perspective of environmental economy. Work in this direction has been going on for over a decade, not only to maintain the region's competitiveness in the tourism market, saturated with "sun and sand" offerings, but also to make this autonomous community a place where residents' lives are not just a constant choice between the false dichotomy development/destruction, stagnation/conservation.

We will briefly cover the Balearics' economic and territorial evolution from before the eruption of tourism into their economic base, through its most critical moments, pointing out the most significant traits, positive and negative, generated in each period. We also wish to refer to the present and the future of the region in light of the new strategies instrumentalized in accordance with the European Regional/Spatial Planning Charter, which are to allow this country to evolve towards a new model of sustainable economic development.

2. The Balearic economic and land-use model in the pretouristic period (1900 – 1950)

Historical sources document that since the eighteenth century the Balearics have been visited by illustrious travellers attracted by their climate and their landscape. But it is not until the beginnings of the twentieth century that one can properly speak of tourism, and a minority and élite tourism at that, as in other classic destinations of the Mediterranean. This period, which in the Balearics we usually call pretouristic and which some authors classify as the stage of social elitism, covers the first half of the twentieth century.

Tourism's effects did not significantly transform the Balearic land-use model in this period, although some measures were taken and some actions carried out which were directly linked to the development and promotion of tourist activity.

The first institution dedicated to the promotion of tourism, "El Fomento del Turismo", was created in 1905, and by the middle of the thirties Mallorca had eighty-eight hotels, among them the veteran Hotel Victoria (1910) and Hotel Mediterráneo (1923). Both are on Palma's *paseo marítimo*, one of the most outstanding features in the city, which has become one of its most prestigious areas. The coasts of other Mallorcan municipalities were not lacking in activity: the renowned Hotel Formentor, on the bay of the same name, was inaugurated in 1929 and the first housing developments were built: Cala d'Or in Santanyí, Palma Nova in Calviá, Alcanada in Alcúdia and Bellavista in S'Arenal, all of them original nuclei of what would later be very densely occupied tourist areas.

In spite of everything, the agrarian way of life, albeit combined with an incipient handicrafts industry, predominated in the Balearics until well into the sixties. The high rate of primary-sector employment (40%), greater than the secondary-sector rate (33.3%) recorded in 1950, only reflects a little-evolved socio-economic structure, in which almost half of the income was generated by agricultural or industrial activities, which furthermore were not sufficiently productive to satisfy the needs of the population, many of whom were forced to emigrate to improve their prospects. This caused negative migratory balances to persist until 1955 and consequent aging of the demographic structure. (Graphic 1)

The dominant economic model in this phase consolidated in turn a land-use model marked by scant development and concentration of population in the municipalities in which a certain economic dynamism was generated, capable of draining surplus labor from rural areas. This was the case in the regional capital, Palma, which in 1950 held 39% of the population; in the two other island capitals Eivissa and Maó, in certain industrial municipalities (Inca, Lloseta, Sòller), and in those that enjoyed notable agricultural productivity thanks to the introduction of innovations in the system of exploitation, as in Sa Pobla (SALVÀ 1999).

Graphic 1 The Balearic Economy in 1950

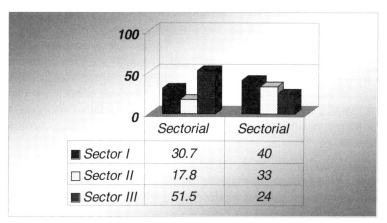

Source: BARCELÓ (1969)

The region's connection with the national and international economic system was maintained through the Balearics' three major ports, those of Palma, Eivissa and Maó, which handled practically all passengers and merchandise. In 1950 they handled around 300,000 passenger movements and 462,000 tons of cargo (1.1 tons per inhabitant). That same year, Palma's small airport of Son Bonet, the region's only international airport in this period, began to evolve, albeit timidly, towards specialization in tourism. The 75,000 passengers recorded are striking enough, all the more so if we consider that they constituted 20% of the national air traffic of the time (Graphic 2).

Graphic 2 Movements trough Mallorca´s Port and Airport (1950)

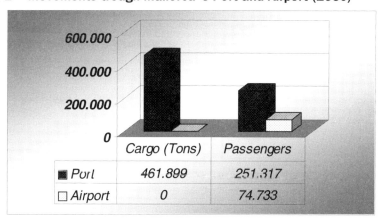

Source: ALCOVER (1969)

3. The transformation of the economic and land-use model (1960 – the 90s)

At the beginning of the sixties the Balearics underwent very strong growth in tourism, a true boom which must be attributed to several factors. Some were endogenous: a rich natural and cultural heritage, the availability of land at low prices, the abundance of labor from the agricultural sector and their location next to the most developed parts of Europe. Other were exogenous: the full economic development of north-western Europe, the establishment in Europe of an economic and land-use model tending to segregate work and leisure areas, and the new demand for vacations on the new, up-and-coming southern periphery, the Mediterranean.

All these previous conditions made the Balearics a tourist destination with enormous potential. The option chosen with respect to the class of tourist desired and the form of growth adopted only increased to their limits all the possibilities for exploiting the product in the most intensive way.

The hardest phase of the growth process was between 1960 and 1973, a year of generalized economic crisis in Europe as a consequence of the first oil crisis. In this period the pressure of tourist demand is reflected in interannual growth over 60%, corresponded to by chaotic development of the offerings, which exceeded 200% interannual growth.

Graphic 3   Evolution of Tourist Places

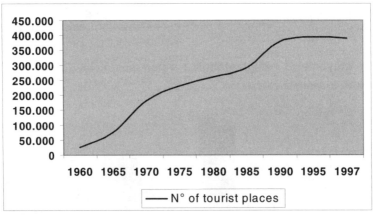

Source: IBATUR (1998)

All of this obviously meant extraordinary pressure on the land, yielding a Defert index, (number of tourist places/inhabitants x 100), of 47 in 1975, almost one place per two inhabitants (Graphic 4)

Graphic 4 Evolution of the Defert index

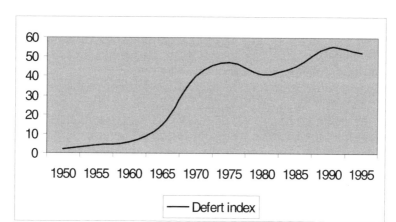

This accelerated transformation came about during the same period in other regions of the country. There were breaks with previous stages at the economic, social and cultural levels, and demographic changes not only in population structure but also in its distribution (DÍEZ QUIDIELLO 1998).

Exterior transportation infrastructures also felt the pressure of tourism. In 1960 Mallorca's air traffic, faced with the incapacity of the old airport of Son Bonet, had to be shifted to the new airport of Son Sant Joan. In 1969 Menorca's new airport was inaugurated and the old one, in operation since 1949, was abandoned. Eivissa's airport, functioning since 1958, entered the international market for the first time. The evolution of the flows handled by these airports between 1960, beginning of the tourism boom, and 1973, beginning of the first crisis, is quite spectacular. In 1962 they reached 700,000 passengers, while in 1973 they exceeded 9,000,000 an average annual increase of approximately 26% (Graphic 5).

Graphic 5 Evolution of air passenger transport in the Balearic

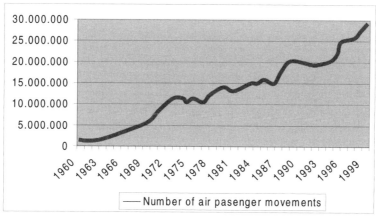

Source: AENA

The interior transportation infrastructures also had to meet the demand pressure, so that in the first years of the sixties many very important actions in this sector had to be undertaken. The islands' first motorway was inaugurated, a stretch of ten kilometres joining Palma with Son Sant Joan airport, which profoundly transformed one of the city's most outstanding areas, the edge of the historic centre next to the sea. Palma's network of major arteries was designed, which included new motorways to allow smooth traffic flow between the capital and the nearest municipalities, Calvià and Llucmajor, the most touristic in those years. It was also in this period that traffic density began to grow rapidly, as a consequence of the great number of automobiles available, which for the first time made the Balearics the region with the highest index of motorization in Spain.

The economic model in these years is marked by the drainage of labor and investments from industry and agriculture into services, marking the beginning of the Balearics' shift into a strongly service-sector economy.

This shift marked the land-use model very significantly. Patterns of settlement began to be reversed, the coast now gaining in value, with a great profusion of touristic and residential settlements, while the inland municipalities lost population and especially endogenous economic dynamism, becoming dependent on the wealth generated on the coast.

Not only did this situation not concern the competent institutions, they counted on and even furthered it through various instruments of development planning. The Balearic Provincial Development Plan, approved in 1973, gave its blessing to the model of a "continuum" of touristic and residential developments along the coasts of the islands.

4. The economic and land-use model of the late twentieth century

In economic terms, the evolution towards the service sector has been positive and spectacular. The Balearics have taken a firm lead since the seventies as the Spanish region with the highest per capita income (around 18,000 pesetas/inhabitant), the highest activity ratio (54.03%, five points over the Spanish average) and the lowest unemployment rate (11%). However, these brilliant economic results hide structural imbalances we will comment on later, when we take up the model's impacts (Graphic 6)

The resulting land-use model has only radicalized its inland/coastal duality. In inland Mallorca only the dynamic axis joining Palma and Alcúdia – which has been maintaining the greatest population densities since the sixties, linked to the industrial development of the el Raiguer area – is still going strong, absorbing part of Palma's extra-municipal expansion. But it is in the coastal municipalities where tourism is most active, such as Calvià, Capdepera, Son Servera, Sòller and Alcúdia in Mallorca, or Sant Antoni de Portmany and Santa Eulària in Eivissa, that the patterns of regional growth are most marked. These are the municipalities that show the greatest population densities and hold most of the more than 500,000 tourist places that make up the region's lodgings. Of these, 265,720 are in Mallorca, 42,798 in Menorca, 77,802 in Eivissa and 7,530 in Formentera.

Graphic 6   GDP and Employment structure in the Balearics (1997)

	Sectorial	Sectorial
■ Sector I	1	3
□ Sector II	16	21
■ Sector III	82	76

Source: Govern Balear

The municipalities of the Serra de Tramuntana and the Pla in Mallorca remain outside this expansive dynamic, sunk in demographic and economic regression, though some of them have recently become engaged in a new mode of tourist activity with offerings of rural tourism and agrotourism. This new offer on the market is allowing some farms to keep cultivating crops and raising animals and has meant the rehabilitation and conservation of an important cultural heritage.

This revaluation of rural areas is very recent. BINIMELIS (1999) says that the process began in the nineties and could redefine the land-use model in the future, especially in Mallorca, where the new forms of occupation of rural land are more widespread. While in these years ample touristic offerings have proliferated in rural areas, these same areas have also seen development in the form of second homes, in demand by Mallorcans as well as foreign residents. All of this, as BINIMELIS says, is nothing other than the extension of urban uses to the impoverished rural sphere. In short, it is another step in the deepening of an economic-territorial model in which the service sector predominates and which is dependent on tourism, referred to "mass", "ecological", "green", or "alternative".

The transportation infrastructures, which allow the land-use dynamic to be maintained, cannot but reflect the imbalances of the model they serve. The autonomous community's road network now has a total length of 2,342 km, of which 49 km are motorways. Although this yields a density of only .5 km/km^2, less than the national average of .7 km/km^2, it is very intensively used, for two reasons. First, the large number of vehicles, which included 423,923 passenger cars in 1995. The Balearics have 59 private vehicles per 100 inhabitants, that is, almost three for every five inhabitants, well over the national average (36 vehicles/100 inhabitants) and any other Spanish regional average. If we consider vehicles of all types, the ratio in the Balearics reaches 90 vehicles/inhabitant, one of the highest in Europe. Another significant fact is that in only six years the number of vehicles registered in the Balearics has quadrupled. Second, the use of roads and streets in the Balearics is very high because of the constant expansion of discretionary transport in tourist activity (excursions, changes of lodging, etc.). But what is most serious is its unbalanced level of service: the large concentrations of traffic around the capital and on the axes connecting it with the principal tourist areas, which mark the unequal occupation of the land, related to its unequal potential, function and capacity to attract; and the seasonal occupation of transportation, with an enormous contrast between the months of low season and high season. In high season, besides changes of lodging and tourist excursions in busses, there is the operation of Spain's largest fleet of rental cars (58,000 vehicles 1999).

The exterior transportation infrastructures, the ports and airports, have borne the brunt of the pressure from tourism and its imbalances still more directly, since they are the entry and exit points for visitors. In 1997 the Balearics' three airports registered around 22,000,000 passengers, an air mobility index (passengers/inhabitants x 100) of 263%, greater than that of any other European Mediterranean region (MARTÍNEZ 1997). Palma's airport, with over 16,000,000 passengers, is among Europe's busiest in international traffic. However, the enormous demand for air travel contrasts with the weak expansion of sea traffic, which handles around 1,000,000 passengers to and from the peninsula, although it handles nearly all cargo traffic. Some 7,000,000 tons pass through the region's ports annually, nine tons per inhabitant.

Besides the traffic with the peninsula, the islands have become one of the favourite stops for cruise ships in the Mediterranean. Over 500,000 passengers call at Palma and Alcúdia (Mallorca); Eivissa, Maó (Menorca); and Cala Sabina (Formentera).

Flows of both passengers and merchandise, whether handled by air or sea, are equally marked by summer seasonality as a consequence of the strong touristic pressure at this time of year. The problem of seasonality is especially serious in the airport system, which is obliged to take on huge proportions to handle peaks of demand in summer which do not exist the rest of the year.

Graphic 7   Movements trough Balearic ports and airports (1997)

	Port	Airport
Cargo (Tons)	7.486.597	32.389
Passengers	557.278	22.999.403

Source: SEGUÍ, MARTÍNEZ (1999)

5. The model of seasonal mass tourism – Its impacts

Seasonal mass tourism, established as the driving force of the Balearic economy in the period described above, has generated a model of regional development which avidly consumes natural resources, land and water among them, at the same time that it causes multiple impacts in other spheres, the social, economic and environmental.

5.1 The land-use model

The land-use model is characterized by the macrocephalic growth of Palma, to the detriment of a more balanced urban network; and the strong duality between coastal municipalities, which present a very progressive demographic and functional dynamic, and those lying inland, clearly regressive. But even within the coastal municipalities themselves a certain dichotomy is in evidence between the traditional town center, usually less populated, and the touristic settlements, usually the centers of highest concentration.

The most evident imbalance in this situation is the scant connection between tourist centers and traditional centers, aggravated by certain characteristics of the former, such as their high rate of occupation, a high density of construction, rarely of architectural quality, and a functional dynamic strongly marked by seasonality.

While coastal development characterized the process of tourist occupation for many years, new patterns of urban occupation have recently appeared. This has meant the colonization of inland areas by second homes and by new touristic offerings, such as rural tourism and agrotourism.

5.2 Water resources

Water is one of the scarcest resources in the Balearics because we have no source other than rain, and even that cannot all be put to use. If we add the region's low rainfall, we can understand the seriousness of the situation.

In spite of the actions undertaken in the sixties to mitigate the supply problems caused by the tourism boom, the enormous growth of demand and the new land uses that have arisen have pushed the situation near its limits. According to the Govern Balear's latest studies, regional demand is some 291 hm^3/year, while the capacity of current hydraulic infrastructures is around 312 hm^3/year. Obviously, this makes the current demand growth rate unsustainable.

This is not the only problem affecting water resources. Some aquifers near flat areas where irrigated agriculture is still practiced (Pla de Sant Jordi, flat areas of Llucmajor-Campos, Sa Pobla-Muro, Eivissa, Sant Antoni and Santa Eulària) are contaminated by nitrites and chlorides. Those on the coast are almost all salinized or in clear danger of salinization by infiltration of sea water as a consequence of overuse. In 1998, according to the Dirección General de Sanidad eighty-one cases of excessive chlorides and eighteen of excessive nitrates were detected in the supply network, and forty-three of each in wells.

To avoid contamination as much as possible, as well as to enable the reuse of wastewater for domestic or agricultural use, the Balearics have a good number of purification plants. Seventy-six are under municipal management, fifty-eight are under the Instituto Balear de Saneamiento (IBASAN), and sixty-eight are private (PERELLÓ 1999).

Their distribution shows a strong relationship with population density, so that it is the most populated and most touristic municipalities that have the most purification plants, generally private in the touristic enclaves.

The salinization problem has been especially serious in Palma and Calvià, two municipalities with high demand, which in particularly dry years have had to resort to importing drinkable water from Tarragona by ship, a measure protested by groups of ecologists. In 1996 6,800,000 tons were brought in in an old oil tanker especially set up for transporting water. The definitive solution to this serious problem, at least in the immediate future, is the imminent start-up of a desalinization plant on Palma's bay to supply drinking water to Palma and Calvià.

5.3 The environment

Besides the transformation of the land-use model, which as one can easily see is constantly being redefined, the environmental impacts on the land have come above all from development. The extension of developments, first on the coast and later in rural areas, the proliferation of golf courses, the extraction of sand from the sea floor to increase the capacity of the beaches, and the constant expansions of infrastructures that must serve ever greater and more mobile populations are the principal actions with strong impact on the land and the principal causes of ecosystem degradation.

We should also point out other types of environmental pollution proper to urban life, the emission of air pollutants, the contamination of marine water, and waste dumping.

Scant industrial development, the predominance of relatively clean installations in general, and more specifically the absence of especially polluting large plants are some of the positive aspects of our islands with respect to the preservation of the environment. However, the effects of the traffic infrastructures, i.e. of the exhaust emitted by ground vehicles and especially by aircraft, are often neglected.

Although the problem of aircraft exhaust is very much under control, the emission of polluting gases is not. Nitrogen oxides, unburned hydrocarbons, sulphur oxides, carbon monoxide and fuel additive residues contribute to the destruction of the ozone layer, the formation of acid rain and the extension of the greenhouse effect, and have negative effects on the health of passengers and airport workers. According to a 1997 report from Friends of the Earth, nitrogen oxides can cause respiratory problems, while unburned hydrocarbons and soot may cause some cancers.

5.4 Solid urban waste

Another problem generated by the pressure of tourism is the production of waste, especially urban waste. The Balearic Islands are sadly a leader in this aspect, with a production of 555 kg/year/inhabitant, well over the average of the countries of the Organization for Economic Cooperation and Development (400 kg/year/inhabitant), and what is worse, 33% of this receives no treatment because it is deposited in uncontrolled dumps (BONO 1998), with the consequent danger of contaminating subsoils and aquifers.

The inventory of solid urban waste dumps in the islands in 1995 and 1996 recorded 172, almost half of them in Mallorca. Only 15% were properly controlled, 44% were clandestine and 41% uncontrolled (PERELLÓ 1999)

In the face of this disturbing situation, the *Solid Urban Waste Management Master Plan*, now being executed, was drawn up, and a policy of selective collection and recycling put into practice, although not sufficiently effective given the inadequacy of installations set up for the treatment, storage, and elimination of this waste. A good example is the incinerator of Son Reus in Palma, whose smoke is a health risk for those living nearby, a danger repeatedly denounced by residents of the most affected municipalities (Palma, Bunyola) and by several ecological institutions.

5.5 The economy

Excessive dependence on a very little-diversified service sector, linked to strongly seasonal tourism, also provokes the seasonality of employment, with the aggravating factor of the destruction of the agricultural fabric and traditional industries. It is worth noting that the service sector generates 82% of the gross regional product, over half of that due to tourist activity, and 76% of the jobs.

All this implies scant control over commercialization of tourism and the export industry and consequently a severe economic dependence on the exterior, to the detriment of the autonomous community's financial capacity (GOVERN BALEAR 1997).

This also implies, as MONTSERRAT (1994) says, a very unstable labor market, marked by seasonality. Unstable because any crisis affecting the countries whence tourists come has direct repercussions on occupation levels, although recovery is very rapid. Marked by seasonality, because the product offered and the demand for it are seasonal. In the Balearics the variation of the active wage-earning population between January and July oscillates about 13%, while the numbest of unemployed drops by more than 40% over this period.

5.6 Society and culture

The autochthonous population, immigrants and tourists' living together has produced a cultural shock and consequent social and cultural changes of all types, as yet insufficiently analyzed. It is worth bering in mind that 34% of the population was born outside the region and 10% of marriages in the Balearics are between a foreigner and a Spanish citizen. The number of permanent European residents in the islands has also increased recently and now represents 10% of the population (88,098 people (P. SALVÀ, *Diari de Balears*, May 9, 1999).

As a striking indicator of tourism's impact on our society, we should note that by year's end thirteen tourists will have passed through the islands for each resident, most during the high season: June, July, August and September. These tourists are generally uninterested in the region's culture or ways of life, and usually maintain their own forms of leisure, customs, and obviously their language, drinks, music, etc.

All this has been slipping into the ways of life of the resident population, enriching the society but also dissolving usages and customs and introducing other habits extraneous to our culture. For example, the disappearance of placenames in favour of others linked to tourist activity (PICORNELL 1994) and the decreasing use of Catalan, the language of the Balearic Islands, especially in the touristic municipalities of the coast and in the principal cities in favour of Spanish and other foreign languages, such as German. Also very important is the progressive transformation of traditional markets into *mercadillos* of souvenirs, knickknacks and poor-quality craft objects almost never produced in the islands, frequented more by tourists than by residents. Finally we should mention the implantation of traditional fairs from other places, such as the *Bierfest* or Seville's April fair, which enjoy greater success every year.

As P. SALVÀ concludes, (*op. cit.*), the European residents are interested in the islands as a refuge but 40% of those who have arrived recently feel no interest or concern for the local culture. SALVÁ says that thanks to new communication technologies, 90% of foreign residents follow news and other programs from their countries of origin.

6. The sustainable development model proposed in the Balearics – Previous measures and the Regional Planning Directives

The urbanization dynamic, fuelled by population pressure, new residential uses stemming from reckless development, and the degradation of overcrowded tourist areas, began to be perceived as problems by the resident population and visitors and denounced as such over a decade ago.

In this context, having assumed full jurisdiction over touristic matters in 1984 with the creation of Spain's autonomous communities, the administration has begun to intervene with various norms and laws to limit growth, improve the touristic offering and conserve natural areas yet unaffected by the impacts of development.

In 1989 the general criteria were approved for drawing up the *Tourist Amenities Development Plan* (POOT) whose prime objective was to favour qualitative growth in a reversal of the traditional policy of favouring quantitative regional development. The actions proposed involve establishing rational limits to growth, to avoid worse conflicts in the region's already precarious ecological balance, as well as seeking the integral recovery of saturated areas. Recovery is fundamentally based on the restoration of balance among the variables that influence carrying capacity (drinking water supply, purification plants, hotels, shops, etc.), but also on the recovery of environmental quality.

The POOT's most striking and novel measure to avoid reckless growth was the establishment of a minimum ratio of 60 m^2 land/1 hotel. This measure is intended to avoid the endemic problem of overcrowding in newly built or growing tourist areas.

In 1991 the *Natural Areas Law* (LEN) went into effect, which although affecting regional tourism development, especially the hypothetical creation of new tourist areas or the surroundings of extant ones, has much greater importance for society and for the land. This law catalogues natural areas of special natural, cultural o scenic interest and establishes various legal statuses for their protection (Table 1). The catalogue of areas protected by the LEN lists more than 100 areas of special scenic interest rich in fauna or flora, covering 34% of the islands' surface. The areas with the highest level of protection, the absolute prohibition of development in any form, are the ANEI (Natural Areas of Special Interest), among which are Natural Parks, National Parks and Natural Reserves.

Referring more explicitly to tourist activity is the *Quality Plan Q*, now being worked on, which affects tourist areas and their surroundings. The "Q" plan began in 1994 and includes three broad lines of action. The first is the *Hotel Amenities Modernization Plan,* which has allowed all the islands' hotels to be renovated and some of the obsolete beds to be eliminated from the market. The second, within the framework of the POOT, introduces the limitation of hotels, specifying a quota in each tourist area. Any new place exceeding the established maximum volume in an area thus entails the disappearance of an existing one. The third line of action, which affects the improvement of the touristic milieu, is structured in various plans and laws. In this way the LEN is applied. The *Sanitation Plan* allows for the treatment of 92% of the wastewater released into the sea. The *Beautification Plans*, on the municipal level, are for functional enrichment of tourist areas with the construction of multi-use facilities, such as auditoriums, sports installations and cultural centers, allowing for the diversification of the local offerings. The *Demolition Plan* aims at the recovery of saturated tourist areas, a process based on the elimination of obsolete hotel buildings and the transformation of their lots into promenades, recreational areas, or social facilities.

Table 1   Protective statuses established by the natural areas law (LEN)

ANEI: Natural areas of special ecological value, declared undevelopable to preserve their singularity or ecological richness.

ARIP: Rural areas of special scenic interest, declared undevelopable to preserve their character.

AAPI: Areas prepared for visitors in landscapes of special interest. Construction is possible here though strongly regulated to preserve the existent natural surroundings.

NATURAL PARK: Areas totally protected and managed in a way that guarantees the preservation of their great natural assets. In the Balearics we have four natural parks: s'Albufera, Mondragó and sa Dragonera in Mallorca and s'Albufera des Grau in Menorca.

NATIONAL PARK: Areas similar to Natural Parks though with national status. The small Cabrera archipelago is one.

RESERVE NATURAL: The natural reserves are ses *Salines* in Eivissa, the islets of es *Freus* and ses *Salines* in Formentera.

Source: IBATUR (1996). *Illes Balears. Guía dels Espais Naturals. Mallorca, Menorca, Eivissa i Formentera.* Instituto Balear de Promoción del Turismo. Conselleria de Turisme. Govern Balear.

The most recently approved measure is the General Tourism Law (1999), which rationalizes and synthesizes all previous tourism legislation. Its general lines are the promotion and quality of the touristic offering, deseasonalization and preservation of the environment. Its basic criteria are: the limitation of tourist places, requiring the elimination of obsolete ones for the concession of new licences; the permanent modernization of tourist establishments; maintaining the POOT in full force; quality control, training; R+D; infrastructure improvements and beautification plans; and the correct use of tourism resources on a basis of respect for environmental conservation and minimization of consumption.

However, as important as these regulations are, we still lacked an overall legal framework that would cover all the land-use components in a global and interrelated form and permit all the sectorial planes to be applied without conflicts or overlapping of authority, a legal framework which began to take shape as the Regional Planning Directives (DOT) in 1995 and 1996.

The autonomous community of the Balearic Islands was one of the first in Spain to develop Regional Planning Directives, approved in 1999, a supramunicipal land-use planning instrument, therefore capable of overcoming the limitations of local planning.

The philosophy governing the global land-use model proposed by the DOT (GOVERN BALEAR 1996, 1997) is inspired by the European Regional/Spatial Planning Charter, and like it, the DOT have the objective of defining a coherent and integrated land-use model, agreed upon by the whole society, that guarantees sustainable development. The DOT are therefore the expression at the regional level of the commitments of the states that participated in the 1992 Rio Summit, i.e., to integrate in their regional development policies the reduction of poverty and protection of the environment as an interrelated and indissociable whole.

In their diagnostic phase the DOT place special emphasis on the imbalances caused by the regional development model of touristic monoculture. However, tourism is not renounced as a base for a sustainable economic model in the future. Rather, it is acknowledged that those endogenous factors that have been able to generate the change in the traditional model (location with respect to the rest of Europe and a rich natural and cultural heritage), as well as the body of professionals and infrastructures that has been taking shape, constitute an excellent base for evolving towards a better future. But it is also made explicit that this new future cannot be the result of the juxtaposition of plans and projects with uncontrolled regional development, at the mercy of exterior fluctuations and interior needs, because this way of managing the land and its resources has been the cause of the obvious territorial, social and economic imbalances in the region. Hence the DOT persistently reiterate the need to configure a global land-use model that is fair, arrived at by consensus, and compatible with a model of sustainable economic development according to Brundtland's commonly accepted definition, that is, satisfying the present generation's needs without thereby compromising the capacity of future generations to satisfy their own. Capable of producing what is necessary, but only that. Limiting itself to replacing the resources consumed. In sum, capable of maintaining a non-decreasing level of wealth.

Starting from this commitment, the sustainable land-use model proposed in the DOT contemplates three broad strategic lines of action. The first groups all those regulations tending to consolidate the physical as base and support of the land-use model. The second is meant to enhance the structuring function of the urban framework. The third is dynamization of the land-use model through management and preservation of the cultural heritage.

6.1 The land

It is proposed to protect valuable natural areas, recover the landscape and treat rural land from a global perspective, not fragmented by the management of various municipalities, through a group of measures and actions. The islands' biodiversity is to be conserved, maintaining the strong protection of the natural areas of special interest catalogued by the LEN.

Another the line of action consists in delimiting different areas with defined "vocations", identifying "units of ecological interest"; "units of scenic interest" and "units of agricultural interest". This classification will allow us to adapt the land-use model to the land, its accommodation capacity and its vocation.

At present, rural land has value exclusively for urbanization and residential development. Speculative pressure has provoked sharp increases in its price. The Govern Balear has therefore recently approved the creation of a land bank for the cultivation of abandoned farms. In this way, farmers, especially young farmers, can be brought into contact with the land's owners.

A third proposal of the DOT is a network of natural recreational areas to satisfy the population's demand for recreational activity, always respecting the "vocation" of the land. Another objective is to promote contact and interrelation of the population with the land and educate them in environmental conscientiousness and participatory behaviour. To accomplish these objectives it is proposed that the intensity of recreational uses be planned below the accommodation capacity of the natural areas, so that they will filter the population for the most fragile and valuable ones.

One of the most complex policy challenges of actions regarding the land derives from the declaration of Menorca as a biosphere reserve in the face of the recent but ever stronger pressure of tourism and development this island is experiencing, which threatens to implant a model of intensive touristic exploitation similar to that suffered by Mallorca and Eivissa.

6.1.1 Menorca, biosphere reserve

Menorca is the only island of the Balearics to undergo socio-economic development compatible with the conservation of its artistic, cultural and environmental heritage. This situation has earned it declaration as a Biosphere Reserve by UNESCO in 1993.

Menorca is practically flat, its only notable elevations being El Toro (350 meters), and the massifs of Santa Àgueda (264 meters), s'Enclusa (274 meters) and ses Penyes d'Egipte, all declared Natural Areas of Special Interest.

As for natural habitats, three large units should be distinguished: the coast, some 290 km with coves and beaches whose dune systems are protected areas of special beauty; the ravines, whose beds hold rich vegetation and along which there are caves harbouring true biological treasures; and wetlands in which dense vegetation and a great diversity of fauna flourish.

The LEN deal with this rich natural heritage in the form of 19 ANEIs occupying 43% of the island's surface (Table 2), one of which, S'Albufera des Grau and Illa d'en Colom, is a Natural Park. In the Balearics as a whole the level of protection is 34% of the surface area.

As for the cultural heritage, the Archaeological Charter of the Balearics attests the high density of archaeological settlements in Menorca, over the average for the Balearics, approximately 1 settlement/km^2.

Table 2   Natural areas of Menorca

Area	Type of protection	Surface
North coast of Ciutadella	ANEI	674 hectare
La Vall	ANEI	3,125 hectare
From es Alocs to Fornells	ANEI	2,556 hectare
Bella Vista	ANEI	129 hectare
From Addaia to s'Albufera	ANEI	1,783 hectare
S'Albufera des Grau	ANEI	1,994 hectare
From s'Albufera to la Mola	ANEI	1,747 hectare
San Isidre-Bisermenya	ANEI	223 hectare
Cala St. Esteve-Caló d'en Rafalet.	ANEI	320 hectare
From Biniparratx to Llucalcari	ANEI	2,016 hectare
Son Bou and the ravine of sa Vall	ANEI	1,212 hectare
From Binigaus to Cala Mitjana	ANEI	1,682 hectare
Southern coast of Ciutadella	ANEI	1,166 hectare
Son Olivaret	ANEI	168 hectare
Camí de Baix (Degollador)	ANEI	9.1 hectare
Santa Àgueda-s'Esclusa	ANEI	2,938 hectare
El Toro	ANEI	2,136 hectare
Penyes d'Egipte	ANEI	2,207 hectare

Source: IBATUR (1996). Illes Balears. Guía dels Espais Naturals. Mallorca, Menorca, Eivissa i Formentera. Instituto Balear de Promoción del Turismo. Conselleria de Turisme. Govern Balear.

Starting from the levels of protection afforded by the LEN, the general objectives now assumed by the DOT centre on the conservation and management of the island's natural heritage, preserving its biodiversity and its ecosystems and seeking the recovery of its environmental quality wherever it has been affected, as well as the management and preservation of its historical heritage, seeking uses that do not degrade it. Obviously such objectives must come about through the participation of the whole society, inculcating a culture of sustainability among the population, that is, rational use of the island's natural resources, and commitment on the part of land managers, administrations and scientific researchers.

6.2   The urban framework

The second line of action is meant to enhance the structuring function of the urban framework. For this, the urban system is ordered as part of the global, interrelated system, in an attempt to break the traditional territorial duality that functionally fractures the territory into two unconnected parts. Another goal is to rebalance the weight of the great structuring nexuses and reinforce the leadership of nuclei of middling supramunicipal influence. This should guarantee the economic viability and physical renovation of inland towns while preserving the identity of traditional population centers. Complementarily, a group of regulations is intended to order urban growth in the new tourist centers. Some of the proposed actions are: clear delimitation of tourist areas; improvement and diversification of the offering; protection of the nature and the environmental quality of these areas; and control and regulation of diffuse development in zones that cannot be urbanized, for the sake of maximal integration of these constructions into the rural landscape.

6.3   Dynamization of the land-use model

The third strategic line of the DOT seeks dynamization of the land-use model through management and preservation of the cultural heritage. As for the dynamizing effect of the cultural heritage, these directives make four proposals. First, the creation of a network of ethnographic parks to allow the conservation and regeneration of the Balearics' cultural and natural heritage; education and sensitization of the population, and the dynamization and economic regeneration of the land through a diversified economic model. Second, integral rehabilitation programs in historical centers, giving priority to those of greatest quality and historic-cultural interest. Third, programs of restoration and revaluation of the cultural heritage as an essential element of strategies of land-use development. Lastly, creation of a network of scenic and cultural routes allowing a different reading and better understanding of the territory, a complementary alternative to the traditional options of sun and sand.

6.4   Infrastructures and facilities

Obviously, it is necessary to place special emphasis on the infrastructures and facilities that allow the islands to be fashioned into an interrelated, global system, offering varied and attractive options, and the DOT are also concerned with this issue.

6.4.1 Transportation infrastructures

Rebalancing the interior transportation infrastructures, the port and airport system, is one of the proposed objectives. The use of Son Bonet airport as a third runway of the modern Son Sant Joan airport or a low-impact airport on the island of Formentera would seem to be sufficient to meet predicted air traffic in the short and middle term.

On the other hand, the Balearics' ports seem to present greater problems given the difficulties of their functional connection with their urban surroundings, as well as the dangers of manipulating fuel products near these surroundings. These are two key issues to be confronted in the future.

6.4.2 Telecommunications. The Balearic Telematics Innovation Strategy (BIT)

The telematics innovation strategy, instrumentalized by the Govern Balear and contemplated in the DOT, is one of the indispensable elements for the Balearics' incorporation into the information society, and should contribute decisively to diversified and ecologically sustainable economic development.

The BIT strategy foresees construction of a large-scale telecommunications network, making possible teleadministration, telemedicine and distance learning applications through such services as electronic mail and videoconferencing. This obviously presupposes the development of new information technologies, but also the extension of telecommunications to all aspects of life.

Two large projects are now underway, the CentreBIT and the Balearic Telematics Innovation Park (ParcBIT). The CentreBIT is meant to act as a true dynamizer of regional development through the promotion and extension of advanced services in sectors as important for society as health, tourism, business and education, while conserving and optimizing the environmental attractiveness capable of attracting new businesses and their highly qualified professionals. The first CentreBIT is in the industrial park of Inca, leader of Mallorca's el Raiguer, and is meant to dynamize this region, which has suffered severe deindustrialization, by attracting new high-technology businesses, providing the training, resources and communications network access these new businesses and their workers need.

The ParcBIT project, a pioneer in the group of BIT actions, may be framed in an extensive network of technopolises which have appeared in recent years. Located in Palma, it is not yet in an advanced phase. It has been designed as a scientific park adjoining the university. According to the plans of architect Richard Rogers, the park will integrate work, leisure and residence with advanced telematics networks. There will be training and research centers and smart homes for its professionals in an advanced residential complex, compatible with the activity of innovative businesses and institutions.

The telematics innovation strategy also extends to the motor of the islands' economy, tourism. The telematics infrastructures, the powerful collection of hotels and the attractiveness of the environment are enormous endogenous assets, upon which a European network of vacations offices could be established, where telework and leisure time could be made compatible, at the family and not just the individual level.

The Balearic Telematics Innovation Institute, created by the Govern Balear, manages many of the BIT strategy projects.

6.4.3 Facilities

The educational, health, sports, cultural, etc. facilities are all questions that by mandate of the DOT must be focused on from a global perspective, a regional frame of reference that allows resources and facilities to be integrally rationalized. The DOT's assessment of these facilities deals with three fundamental elements that explain their distribution: the autonomous community's division into islands, concentration in Mallorca and the preponderance of the services sector in the Balearics' economic structure.

On the basis of these structural premises, we can affirm that the level of facilities in the Balearics is above our basic needs and in some cases reaches the demand levels of the most developed societies. However, in the highest-level facilities, such as the university or large hospitals, the effect of territorial division is very negative, and is aggravated by the influx of tourists in summer.

A more balanced geographic distribution, correct evaluation of the effects of the transient population and more fluid intraregional connections are the challenges the DOT takes on with respect to health facilities.

With the university facilities, concentrated in Palma for demographic reasons, the problem derives from territorial division, which obliges students to travel from the smaller islands to Mallorca, which thus enters into competition with other destinations outside the archipelago. This problem can be solved only through strategies that make transportation more flexible and less expensive and develop new information technologies. The Campus Extens distance learning project is in fact now functioning through master classes with videoconferences and tutorials via Internet and its various resources such as electronic mail and chats. Thanks to this project students from Eivissa and Menorca can earn some of the degrees offered by the UIB from home.

7. Two cases of sustainable management.

7.1 The "Agenda 21" and the municipality of Calvià (Mallorca)

That the DOT establish for the first time an overall framework of coordinated, global actions to achieve a model of sustainable unitary development does not mean that municipalities do not have a very important role to play in the project. What it means the beginning of a new form of local planning, more consistent and with commitments beyond the limits of each municipality. In fact, the latest and most direct application of the Rio commitments is in the "Local Agendas", that is, the group of actions the municipalities can and must carry out. Currently three tourist areas have "Environmental Quality Action Plans" which will be technical support for implanting the "Agenda Local 21" in 10 Balearic municipalities.

The fundamental difference of these Agendas from the old town planning regulations is that municipalities are involved in integrated, global sustainable development, benefiting not only their own localities, in which they must seek interrelation between development and sustainability, but also thinking of the global land-use system.

Calvià, the most touristic municipality of the Balearic Islands and one of the Mediterranean's most important, was the first municipality of the islands to apply the Agenda 21. For this reason it will serve us as a case study in the new proposals and forms of sustainable tourism growth at the municipal level.

The evolution of Calvià is a paradigm of the evolution of the Balearics: direct, accelerated transition from rural life to the service sector; a brutal increase in development; very heavy immigration; overspecialization in tourism; scant and difficult connection among its twelve population centers; a break between the coast and inland areas; obsolete hotels; and environmental deterioration due to overexploitation, although it is one of the richest municipalities in Spain.

Calvià's "Agenda Local 21" includes 10 broad lines of action:

---

(1) Contain human pressure, limit growth and favour the complete rehabilitation of the land and the coast.

(2) Favour integration, amity and the quality of life of the resident population.

(3) Preserve the natural heritage of the land and sea and promote the creation of a regional ecotax on tourists, to be spent on the environment.

(4) Recover the historic, cultural and natural heritage.

(5) Promote the complete rehabilitation of the residential and touristic population centers.

(6) Improve Calvià as a tourist destination: replace growth with sustainable quality, seek to increase per-visitor spending and balance the tourist seasons.

(7) Improve public transportation and favour walking and riding bicycles between and within population centers.

(8) Introduce sustainable management into the key environmental quality sectors: water, energy and waste.

(9) Invest in human and knowledge resources, dynamize and diversify the economic system.

(10) Innovate in municipal government and expand the capacity of joint public and private investment.

Source: AJUNTAMENT DE CALVIÀ (1997)

Over time, these guidelines should take shape in concrete programs of action. For the moment, a series of immediate actions has been worked out. The first is to ensure sustainability through the General Development Plan now under debate. The other proposed actions are to deal with resources, the environment and the municipality's economic diversification in the near future.

Thus a process of rationalizing recourse consumption has begun, stabilizing the consumption of water, implementing a plan of energy saving and solid waste reduction through recycling and reuse as well as raising the awareness of the resident population and tourists through campaigns of rationalizing water use, and the creation of the Green Office 21 for correctly advising citizens.

Moratoria are established on roadways of significant impact and on major construction on the coast, and a pilot plan is proposed for conservation of the beaches. A business "nursery" has been created and incentives are expanded for Small and Medium-sized Businesses (PIMES). A plan of dynamization of the rural world has begun, among whose measures is the *Rural Initiatives in Calvià* prize. Finally, there is a series of measures making connections: finishing the Passeig Calvià, a major axis exclusively for pedestrians and cyclists, which brings urban areas into contact with the municipality's rural and natural areas, and the improvement of public transport services.

One of the Agenda Local 21's most innovative proposals, meant for financing environmental management, is the ecotax on tourists. This would be a tax applicable throughout the region, about 10 € in high season and 6 € in low season, to be paid by all visitors and tourists in the Balearics, with the resident population obviously exempt. Estimated annual revenues of over ptas 15,000,000 could go towards financing all the actions foreseen, some of which are quite expensive, such as demolition, the acquisition of landmark country estates, rezoning land as undevelopable and the promotion of winter tourism, among others.

7.2 Environmental hotel management – Hotels RIU

One of the basic premises in the DOT to make the project of sustainable growth a reality is the participation of all social agents. One of these agents, very important for the project's correct functioning, is the hotel sector, since a good part of environmental resource management and appropriate land use depends on the hotels and their guests.

Most of the islands' hotels and hotel chains have become involved in the "Ecotur Instalaciones" project to set up environmental management systems in these establishments. By way of example we will cite Hotels RIU, one of the Balearics' most important chains, also present in many of the world's most important tourist destinations.

Hotels RIU have been very intensively involved for many years in managing their hotels in a way compatible with the environment. They have done so through training courses for their managers. Part of their training programs is dedicated to environmental issues, such as the environmental management course within the Nova program of the Ministry of Labour and Social Affairs, taught in Mallorca in 1997, or the course "Tourism and Protection of the Environment" in 1998, which covered such aspects as health, hygiene and the environment.

This hotel chain has also participated actively in various events related with sustainable tourism. It was one of the sponsors of the "World Conference on Sustainable Tourism Lanzarote '95", in the framework of UNESCO's Man and Biosphere program. It also sponsored the "Nattour '96" convention, which convened experts from all over the world in the Canary Islands to analyze tourism's impact on the environment.

A third area of concern is the management of its hotels, in which they have been progressively applying many of the measures that contribute to the establishments' correct functioning in a context of respect for the environment. Below we cite some of the most striking measures applied to their hotels in the Balearics, many generalized throughout the chain.

7.2.1 Waste reduction and treatment

In 1997 all RIU hotels instituted the "ecological breakfast", which meant items were loosely rather than individually packaged. This has enormously reduced waste from aluminium and plastic packaging, and has eliminated plastic bags and containers for individual portions. The estimated reduction amounts to some 5,100 kg of plastic waste per year throughout the chain, around 20,000,000 individual packages (for milk, yoghurt, butter and jam).

Along the same lines, they have eliminated the use of plastic plates, glasses and flatware, except in places where legal safety measures require them, such as beside swimming pools. In these cases the plastic glasses used are reusable.

The waste produced, about 11 litres/stay, is sorted, allowing recycling of paper and cardboard as well as the reuse of glass, since most of the glass containers used are returnable.

7.2.2 Collection and reuse of problematic materials

The hotels of the RIU chain take special care with the oils used in their kitchens. In all the RIU hotels in the Balearics used cooking oil is selectively collected, so that it is never introduced into the sewer system, avoiding pollution and making possible its industrial reuse. Printer toners are also recycled.

7.2.3 Water consumption and purification

The RIU chain's current water-conservation policy includes four broad lines. First, making guests aware of the issue, with information and suggestions on water-saving measures in six languages. Second, reuse of treated water on gardens and golf courses. Third, application of techniques and devices allowing water consumption to be reduced to the minimum, such as drip irrigation in gardens, flow meters in toilet tanks, and installation of low-volume bathtubs and low-flow showerheads. All the water used by these hotels is treated by their own or municipal plants.

7.2.4 Energy consumption

To avoid unnecessarily increasing electrical energy consumption, all the hotels of the RIU chain use low-wattage lightbulbs. Furthermore, all the general lights are programmed, as are the door switches in the rooms and the air-conditioning systems.

7.2.5 Recycled paper

Another way of contributing to ecological hotel management is the use of recycled paper. Hoteles RIU uses recycled paper wherever possible, for example in the bathrooms and for the wrappers of the welcome products.

The internal management of the hotels and headquarters uses basically recycled paper. Photocopier paper, envelopes for internal and external correspondence, and customer response forms are all made of recycled paper.

8. Sustainable tourism and academic activity

The involvement of the Universitat de les Illes Balears and of professionals in search of constant improvements in the touristic product led the university and the Govern Balear to create, at the beginning of the nineties, the School of Hospitality and Tourism, responsible for the training of new generations of professionals. Besides the Hospitality studies, handled by the Govern Balear, the UIB now awards the "Touristic Businesses and Activities Technical" diploma and the second-cycle bachelor's degree in Tourism.

This training agrees with that objective in which all the social agents are involved, the achievement of a sustainable tourism model. Here we should draw attention to the Govern Balear's Tourism Research and Technology Centre (CITTIB), an institution with the responsibility of coordinating and developing research in the discipline of tourism. It now has underway a good number of projects related to environmental issues.

The School of Hospitality and Tourism has been the site of various events, meetings and congresses in which the relationship between tourism and the environment has been the object of analysis. The latest of these, and perhaps the furthest-reaching, was the seminar "The development of sustainable tourism and its relations with land-use planning" on May 26 and 27, 1999, organized by the Council of Europe, the Spanish Ministry of the Environment and the Govern Balear.

This seminar brought together authorities such as the president of the Autonomous Community of the Balearic Islands, the Spanish Minister of the Environment; the Deputy Director of the Environment of the Council of Europe; professionals representing the World Tourism Organization, and tour operators, as well as scientists and researchers from various institutions working in the field of environment, land use and tourism education. The debates and conclusions of all these parties are the source of the lines to develop in the European Conference of Ministers Responsible for Regional Planning, to take place in Hanover in 2000.

The document summing up the seminar and laying out its provisional conclusions points towards these lines. First, it reflects on the growing importance of tourism in Europe and its influence on the economy, environment, and resources. Consequently, it places emphasis on the need for a sustainable orientation in European tourism based on coherent land-use policies. The relationship tourism-land-environment is one of the document's principal foci for reflection. It concludes with a series of points referring to specific policies developed or planned for a new orientation towards the sustainability and quality of tourism in Europe.

The promotion of tourism studies and the Universitat de les Illes Balears' commitment to the sustainable development model, and more specifically to the struggle to transform the touristic model are expressed in other actions, as witnessed by the UIB's recent awarding of an honorary doctorate to the eminent professor JAFAR JAFARI (1999). DR. JAFARI, an authority on tourism, normally teaches and researches at the University of Wisconsin-Stout (USA) although during academic year 1998/1999 he taught in the UIB's School of Hospitality and Tourism as a visiting professor.

In the speech he gave on the occasion of his investiture, JAFARI provides an interesting review of the evolution of thought about tourism, its process of becoming a scientific discipline, and its future as an industry. He lingers over the Spanish tourism sector and does a special analysis of tourism in the Balearics, developed in various points, some of which we extract below because in our opinion the summarize very clearly the reality and the debate, the challenges and the proposals of this sector and its implications for the model of sustainable development to which we are committed.

With respect to sustainable development JAFARI asks: *"What would further tourism growth and development do to the balance of this important ecosystem? How much tourism development is too much? Where on this island or elsewhere in Spain is this balance maintained, who is regulating and policing it, what progress has so far been made in making tourism development sustainable in this ecosystem?"*

He also addresses the point of view of the host population: *"Any tourism development, to be sustainable, must put peoples and their whole philosophy of life in the center. To what extent is this host population prepared to accommodate tourism? In their mind, how many tourists are too many? How about the 'chemistry' between the host and guest? ... Which designated agency is charged with studying this chemistry, in order to introduce measures that can benefit the host, the guest and the whole sociocultural and natural settings – called the Balearic Islands by outsiders but home to insiders?"*

The author concludes singling out the role of the government and the whole Balearic people: *"No strategies will work unless those who hold a stake in tourism are prepared to assume their respective positions in this industry. Education and training programs, tailored for all levels, private and public, are needed in order to manage a sustainable tourism industry which is responding to the needs of the host population and their visitors. As such, the UIB Tourism School is playing a survival role in the Balearic Islands, which depend on the tourism business. The school is educating and preparing the very workforce which will be determining the shape of tourism and thus the future of the islands."*

9. Summary and conclusions

At the beginning of the sixties the Balearics underwent very strong growth in tourism, a true boom which must be attributed to several factors. Some were endogenous: a rich natural and cultural heritage, the availability of land at low prices, the abundance of labor from the agricultural sector and their location next to the most developed parts of Europe. Other were exogenous: the full economic development of north-western Europe, the establishment in Europe of an economic and land-use model tending to segregate work and leisure areas, and the new demand for vacations on the new, up-and-coming southern periphery, the Mediterranean.

All these previous conditions made the Balearics a tourist destination with enormous potential. The option chosen with respect to the class of tourist desired and the form of growth adopted, only increased to their limits all the possibilities for exploiting the product in the most intensive way.

Although this model of touristic development has favoured extraordinary economic expansion, it has also had its costs. Imbalances in the economic structure, in social habits, in territorial dynamics and in natural habitats are the consequence of a feverish development that has seemed to ignore the limitations of the resources growth feeds upon.

In economic terms, the evolution towards the service sector has been positive and spectacular. The Balearics have taken a firm lead since the seventies as the Spanish region with the highest per capita income, the highest activity ratio and the lowest unemployment rate. The resulting land-use model has only radicalized its inland/coastal duality. Recently the revaluation of rural areas has begun through a new type of development in the form of second homes, in demand by Mallorcans as well as foreign residents. This constitutes the extension of urban uses to the impoverished rural sphere.

The transportation infrastructures, which allow the land-use dynamic to be maintained, cannot but reflect the imbalances of the model they serve. The exterior transportation infrastructures, the ports and airports, have borne the brunt of the pressure from tourism and its imbalances most directly, since they are the entry and exit points for visitors. However, not only the economy and the land-use model show the impact of tourism, but the islands' environment, society, demographics and culture are also affected.

In recent years, the increasing awareness of social agents and institutions, as well as the ever more urgent demand, have forced the reconsideration of the regional economy from the perspective of environmental economy. Work in this direction has been going on now for over a decade, not only to maintain the region's competitiveness in the tourism market, saturated with "sun and sand" offerings, but also to make this autonomous community a place where residents' lives are not just a constant choice between the false dichotomy development/destruction, stagnation/conservation.

In this context, having assumed full jurisdiction over touristic matters in 1984 with the creation of Spain's autonomous communities, the administration has begun to intervene with various norms and laws to limit growth, improve the touristic offering and conserve natural areas yet unaffected by the impacts of development. The Regional Planning Directives (DOT), approved in 1999, should become a land-use planning instrument capable of overcoming the limitations of local planning. The positive expectations they generated in their analytic and diagnostic phase, during which the criterion of sustainability was very much present, have not been completely met in its final approval.

Since it is necessary to create a sustainable tourism industry that responds, as JAFARI says, to the needs of residents and visitors to maintain the Balearics' levels of economic competitiveness, the concept of sustainability is beginning to be introduced in some hotels and at the municipal level. This means that municipalities are also involved in integrated, global development, benefiting not only their own localities, in which they must seek interrelation between development and sustainability, but also in regard to the global land-use system.

Bibliography

ALCOVER GONZÁLEZ, R. (1969): Vías de comunicación. In: Baleares y su desarrollo económico. Financial magazine. 17-36. Banco de Vizcaya. Bilbao.

ATLES DE LES ILLES BALEARS (1999). CD. Universitat de les Illes Balears. Palma.

AJUNTAMENT DE CALVIÀ (1997): Calvià Agenda Local 21. La sostenibilidad de un Municipio Turístico. Plan de Acción. Calvià.

ASOCIACIÓN AMIGOS DE LA TIERRA (1997): Tráfico aéreo y cambio climático, Madrid.

BARCELÓ PONS, B. (1969): Problemática del sector agrario. In: Baleares y su desarrollo económico. Financial magazine. 17-36. Banco de Vizcaya. Bilbao.

BINIMELIS, J.; GINARD, A.; SEGUÕ, J.Mª. (1999) Le tourisme rural dans la dernière etape du nouveau modèle territorial de l'île de Majorque. Insula. International Journal of Island Affairs. Special number. February 1999. Paris.

BONO MARTÍNEZ, E. (1998) La política medioambiental en España. In: MELLA MARQUEZ, J.M. (COORD.). Economía y Política regional en España ante la Europa del Siglo XXI. Asociación Española de Ciencia Regional. Madrid. Akal Textos. pp. 608-635.

CLADERA CLADERA, J. (1993): La reconversión de las zonas turísticas saturadas. El caso de Baleares. La formació, la rehabilitació i les noves modalitats turístiques. III Jornades de Geografia del Turisme. UIB. Palma.

DÍEZ QUIDIELLO, J. (1998): Reflexiones sobre las tendencias del desarrollo económico y la sostenibilidad. In: Boletín de la Asociación de Geógrafos Españoles. No. 26. Murcia-Madrid. Asociación de Geografos Españoles. 1st trimester.

GOVERN BALEAR (1996): Directrius d'Ordenació Territorial. Hipótesi del Model Territorial. Conselleria d'Obres Públiques i Ordenació del Territori. Palma.

GOVERN BALEAR (1997): Directrius d'Ordenació Territorial. Anàlisi i Diagnòstic. Conselleria d'Obres Públiques i Ordenació del Territori. Palma.

JAFARI, JAFAR (1999): Tourism assuming its scholarly position. A retrospective and prospective overview. Given on the occasion of Jafari's investiture with an honorary doctorate at the Universitat de les Illes Balears. Palma. 18 May 1999.

MARTÍNEZ REYNÉS, Mª.R. (1997): Transporte aéreo y turismo en Mallorca. Análisis jerárquico y funcional. Unpublished doctoral thesis. Universitat de les Illes Balears. Palma.

MARTÍNEZ REYNÉS, Mª.R. (1999): Espais turístics. In: Atles de les Illes Balears (1999). CD. Universitat de les Illes Balears. Palma.

MARTÍNEZ REYNÉS, Mª.R. (1999): Població ocupada i desocupada. In: Atles de les Illes Balears (1999). CD. Universitat de les Illes Balears. Palma.

MAYOL, J.; MACHADO, A. (1992): Medi Ambient, Ecologia i Turisme a les Illes Balears. Ed. Moll. Palma.

Montserrat Moll, A. (1994): Turisme i ocupació a les Balears. In: Turisme, Societat i Economia a les Balears. Fundació Emili Darder, Palma. pp. 45-50.

Perell Felani, G. (1999): Infraestructures de Sanejament. In: Atles de les Illes Balears (1999). CD. Universitat de les Illes Balears. Palma.

Picornell Bauzi, C. (1994): Els impactes del turisme. In: Turisme, Societat i Economia a les Balears. Fundació Emili Darder, Palma. pp. 11-34.

Rivero C; Salvá, P.A. (1998): La evolución dinámica de los archipiélagos. In: MELLA MÁRQUEZ, J.M. (COORD.). Economía y Política regional en España ante la Europa del Siglo XXI. Asociación Española de Ciéncia Regional. Madrid. Akal Textos. pp. 206-237.

Salvà Tomàs, P.J. (1999): Població. In: Atles de les Illes Balears (1999). CD. Universitat de les Illes Balears. Palma.

Seguí, J.Mª; Martínez, Mª.R. (1999): Els Transports. In: Atles de les Illes Balears (1999). CD. Universitat de les Illes Balears. Palma.

Seguí, J.Mª; Martínez, Mª.R (1999): Comunicacions i Telecomunicacions. In: Atles de les Illes Balears (1999). CD. Universitat de les Illes Balears. Palma

Seminar of the Council of Europe (1999): El desarrollo del turismo sostenible y sus relaciones con la Ordenación del Territorio. Synthesis and Conclusions.

Ximeno Roca, F. (1998): Del concepte a la pràctica. El desenvolupament de l'Agenda 21. In: Eines per a una gestió municipal cap a la sostenibilitat. Diputació de Barcelona. Àrea

Cross-Border Cooperation: The Example of EUREGIO EGRENSIS

GABI TROEGER-WEIß

1. Introduction, or
New framework for cross-border cooperation

Cross-border development as much as cooperation and partnership on a national and international level are among the vast challenges facing Europe at the turn of the millennium. One of the most powerful challenges to meet for the borderland areas between Germany, the Czech Republic and Poland will arise from the EU's expansion to the east. These borderland areas will be afflicted much more than other regions by the spatial and sectoral effects deriving from the EU's expansion. In the intermediate and long term, the advantages and opportunities will outweigh the disadvantages and risks.

What risks and opportunities are we talking about?

1.1 Risks for the german borderland areas caused by the EU's expansion to the East

When it comes to the German borderland areas, represented here by the Bavarian border region to the Czech Republic, the following risks caused by the EU's expansion to the east have to be taken into account:

- Risks for the competitiveness of the (Bavarian) borderland along the Czech border and its economy mainly due to significantly different levels of costs and wages

- Risk of significant regional and structural political turbulences caused by the EU's high sponsorship quotas in the new member countries (the EU strives to declare the borderlands of Poland and the Czech Republic first-priority areas/Objective 1 regions, a fact that will substantially influence investors' locational preferences)

- Risk of rising pressure on the (Bavarian) job market especially in the borderland areas: experts estimate that some 1.5 million gainfully employed persons of all Central and Eastern European countries are willing to take up work in the Western European EU countries; as for the Bavarian job market, an increasing interest in Czech employees can already be observed, a fact which is connected with job market-related structural effects of the economic structural change in the Czech Republic as well as in Poland (example: The District of Hof's Employment Exchange currently has 500 Czech employees registered who commute to the Bavarian borderland every day)

- Risk of migration of business enterprises by relocation from German locations into the Central and Eastern European countries or by new business starts in the CEE-countries due to the lower associated employer outlays and the current social and environmental standards which are not likely to change for quite some time

- Risk of an outflow of purchasing power, especially in the service sector (e.g. health services) and the retail trade due to very low price levels
- Risk of a shift of European infrastructure investments towards the new member countries which have a lot to catch up on in the way of e.g. transportation infrastructure or supply and waste disposal infrastructure

1.2 Opportunities deriving from the EU's expansion to the east

However, in spite of all the risks involved for those living and doing business in the borderland areas, the opportunities should not be forgotten. For the (Bavarian) borderlands, the EU's expansion to the east represents a chance to shape the future. The following ideas will be briefly outlined:

- There is a chance that attractive cross-border economic and high- and middle-tech regions will result with enjoy of international popularity
- a chance that new enterprises will settle in these economic regions perceiving the sales opportunities on the consumer and capital goods markets in the CEE-countries, companies which will be competitive due to the possibilities of compensatory pricing on an international level (opening up new potential markets and sources of supply)
- a chance for the development of new labor markets, so that employees on both sides of the border may profit from job vacancies
- a chance that cross-border service regions will be established and focus on high quality services in the field of traffic and transportation, logistics, international distribution and marketing
- a chance that cross-border tourism, health, and activity regions will be established (e.g. within the Three-Country-Corner Bavaria-Saxony-Bohemia with altogether 16 spas and health resorts, many of which are world-famous)
- a chance to set up joint projects for developing and expanding infrastructure, e.g. in the field of transport infrastructure (such as transnational railway and traffic projects), energy, or telecommunications (such as the vision of cross-border teleregions)
- a chance for the development of a commonly shared living space, including manifold relations and interconnections on both sides of the border, for instance in the field of recreation, culture, social contacts, or sports

The Three-Country-Corner Bavaria-Saxony-Bohemia, representing an important link between Central and Eastern Europe, was offered completely new chances and possibilities for development since the unification of the two German States and the opening of the borders to Eastern Europe. These opportunities often have their roots in the historic background of the region.

Referring now to the Three-County-Corner Bavaria-Saxony/Thuringia-Bohemia, a concrete case of cross-border cooperation on a regional and municipal level will be outlined in the following.

2. Development and structure of cross-border cooperation – the example of EUREGIO EGRENSIS

2.1 Development of cross-border cooperation in the Three-Country-Corner Bavaria-Saxony-Bohemia

The Three-Country-Corner Bavaria-Saxony-Bohemia can look back upon several centuries of common history. Until the borders were closed after World War II, this region was embedded in a network of very close social, economic, and cultural relations and interconnections. Northeast Bavaria, West Bohemia, and the southern part of Saxony once formed a commonly shared living space and economic region in the heart of Europe. The area East Upper Franconia/Saxonian Vogtland/West Bohemia, for instance, marked one of the most important centers of the textile industry in the world before World War II.

These interconnections were destroyed though by the political changes resulting from the second World War and the subsequent redrawing of the borders. Each part of the area developed independently from its neighboring regions, a fact that caused various problems and lead to the origin of different structures.

Due to the opening up of Europe some 10 years ago, the Three-Country-Corner is now given the chance to re-initiate historic connections at the boundary between Central and Eastern Europe, and to establish new common bonds for the advantage of everyone.

The basic philosophy of EUREGIO EGRENSIS is to work for understanding and tolerance by the means of peaceful and friendly cooperation across the borders of the Free State of Bavaria, the Free State of Saxony, and the Czech Republic. In the spirit of good neighborliness and friendship this cross-border region strives to promote and coordinate trans-border cooperation in the entire Three-Country-Corner, trying to boost the development of the region in all its districts.

When EUREGIO EGRENSIS was first founded in 1992/93 as one of 120 Euroregions in Europe (and the first one in Bavaria) it was redefined until 1994. The Bavarian Government provided the build-up financing by means of the EU joint initiative INTERREG I, which, in combination with the membership fees, allowed the Bavarian office as well as the Bavarian and common boards of EUREGIO EGRENSIS to be set up.

An important theoretical step during EUREGIO EGRENSIS' initial phase consisted of the possibility to participate in the preparation of the Trilateral Development Concept, which was worked out by Bavaria, Saxony, and Bohemia under the auspices of the Bavarian State Ministry of Rural Development and Environmental Matters.

This development concept contributed significantly to the subsequent developmental stage of EUREGIO EGRENSIS. Since 1994, this phase is being used to create EUREGIO EGRENSIS' very own profile of responsibilities, and to define an independent area of responsibilities which does not interfere with already existing institutions and organizations.

The realization of concrete cross-border projects, or at least of projects and measures that show any cross-border effects, has been a priority ever since. Of particular interest is the fact that EUREGIO EGRENSIS picks out projects and measures which are innovative and creative and therefore especially important for the regional and municipal cross-border development of the Three-Country-Corner Bavaria-Saxony/ Thuringia-Bohemia.

2.2 Geographical dimensions and organizational structure of EUREGIO EGRENSIS

The internal structure of EUREGIO EGRENSIS includes the Bavarian regions of Eastern Upper Franconia, and the northern part of the Upper Palatinate, the Saxonian regions of the Vogtland area, the Western Ore Mountains, and East Thuringia, as well as the Czech Districts of Karlsbad (Karlovy Vary), Falkenau (Sololov), Eger (Cheb), and Tachau (Tachov) – altogether an area of approximately 17,000 km^2 with almost two million inhabitants.

As for its organizational structure, EUREGIO EGRENSIS has a broad foundation, thus providing good conditions for its fundamental task – managing cross-border projects. Almost all groups of society are integrated in EUREGIO EGRENSIS, i.e. in addition to the communities representing the pillars of EUREGIO EGRENSIS, representatives from the areas of administration, politics, business, science, and education join in as well: chambers, business or other associations, interest groups for culture or sports, cultural organizations, banks, enterprises, churches, unions, and individual persons are interconnected within EUREGIO EGRENSIS.

This broad membership-structure is a fundamental precondition for the realization of EUREGIO initiatives, projects and measurements; wide acceptance of the cooperation can only be achieved by the integration of regional and municipal partners.

As for the structure of the various subgroups involved in EUREGIO EGRENSIS, technical concerns and projects are handled

- in the Common Presidential Board
- in the presidential boards of the three syndicates
- in the common work groups
- in the work groups of the three syndicates, and
- in cross-border project teams (e.g. project team "Student Exchange", or project team "Long Distance Cycling Trail")

3. Material dimensions of cross-border cooperation – the example of EUREGIO EGRENSIS

3.1 Conceptual foundations

A solid conceptual basis was required to provide a firm material foundation and theoretical orientation for cross-border cooperation. Available since 1994, it consists of the "Trilateral Development Concept Bavaria-Saxony-Bohemia" and the "Regional Programme of Action for the Three-Country-Corner Bavaria-Saxony-Bohemia". Both concepts were initiated and decisively supported by the Bavarian Ministry for Rural Development and Environmental Matters; in the current INTERREG II Period they represent an important frame of action and orientation for the work of EUREGIO EGRENSIS as well as for the activities of communities in the Three-Country-Corner.

Furthermore, both concepts provided the foundation for the set up of an operational program concerning the Bavarian-Czech borderlands. This operational program, worked out in detail under the direction of the Bavarian Ministry for Economy, Transportation, and Technology, makes it possible to apply for and provide of means of conveyance for the proposed measures of cross-border cooperation from EU-program, especially from the EU-Program called INTERREG II.

3.2 Regional and project management as foundation for cross-border cooperation

Within EUREGIO EGRENSIS, present theoretical orientation and focal points of cross-border work aim at the realisation of concrete measures and projects (cross-border regional and project management).

Regional and realization management, representing a new attempt at (cross-border) regional and municipal development, include the following objectives within framework of EUREGIO EGRENSIS:

- Project management, i.e. the realization of measures and projects in order to strengthen municipal and regional development
- Information management, i.e. the transmission and exchange of information, especially consultation about the EU (information on European Development Programs)
- Conflict management in order to solve cross-discipline and/or interregional or municipal problems (contribution to reach an agreement)
- Establishment of relations and connections as well as arrangement of meetings for partners who share the same or similar interests and wish to profit from an innovative and creative background
- Use of financial resources especially on the European level
- Regional marketing and public relations work

In their effort to accomplish these objectives, the regional and project management is guided by the following principles:

(1) Partnership between state and municipal institutions

This attempt is based on the conviction that cross-border cooperation in general, but the realization and project management in particular, depend on intense support on the part of government institutions.

(2) Realization of innovative projects and measures – EUREGIO EGRENSIS as a regional innovative forge

EUREGIO EGRENSIS sets out to realize especially the innovative projects and measures and those that reach beyond municipal borderlines. Projects in the field of close-to-public infrastructure (e.g. the modernization of a youth hostel), which could be realized so far without the EUREGIO EGRENSIS' help, will not need its support in the future. In contrary, many projects which are presently being discussed on the municipal and regional level require a trilateral and particularly inter-municipal point of view. Here, EUREGIO EGRENSIS is challenged to support the realization of such projects.

(3) Readiness to take over project sponsorship

Due to the structure of cross-border and inter-municipal projects, it is not always possible to find independent project sponsors in a flexible and short-handed way. Therefore, in order to realize these projects EUREGIO EGRENSIS feels a growing need to take over project sponsorships in cooperation with private and/or public sponsors. In this context the planned qualification offensive financed by means of the European Social Funds (ESF) can be mentioned as an example. On account of the structural situation of the labor market it has been called for by numerous decision units, but a project sponsor could not be found. Nevertheless, to realize this necessary project EUREGIO EGRENSIS has accepted an independent sponsorship during the first stage. After the startup phase it was transferred to a Euroregional R&D company.

(4) Regional management by means of project partnerships

Because of the scarce personnel and financial resources, the exclusive realization of projects by EUREGIO EGRENSIS should be the exception rather than the rule. Ideally, EUREGIO EGRENSIS considers itself a driving force and initiator of projects and a project attendant during the realization phase. EUREGIO EGRENSIS is also willing to act as a project partner, with project partnership being defined as a commonly shared material and financial responsibility for a project (e.g. with regional enterprises, media etc.).

(5) Acceptance of regional responsibility through regional political initiatives

Another guiding principle of EUREGIO EGRENSIS' work can be seen in the acceptance of regional political responsibility. In this context, EUREGIO EGRENSIS considers itself a voice for the regional and municipal interests of all participating communities.

Its regional political engagement is presently focussed on the integration of municipal interests into the framework set by the realization of the EU Joint Initiative INTERREG II and the preparation of the Joint Initiative III, but it strives as well to strengthen the location of Northeast Bavaria, an attempt made necessary by the border to three neighbors with extremely favorable local conditions (wage levels in the Czech Republic, high sponsorship quotas in Saxony and Thuringia).

(6) Integration into regional networks and intensification of regional cooperation

The integration into regional networks and the improvement of regional cooperation represents another important aspect of EUREGIO EGRENSIS' work. Specified in detail this implies

- the collaboration/participation in the Syndicate of European Border Regions (AGEG) including the protection of interests and collecting of information on a European level

- membership in the PHARE Committee under the direction of the Federal Economics Ministry and the Czech Economics Ministry, offering the opportunity to codetermine decisions on cross-border projects on the Czech side

- Conclusion of a cooperation agreement with the Regional Association Päijät-Häme and support of the establishment of Euroregions along the Finn-Russian-Baltic borders

3.3 Projects and measures of cross-border cooperation

The realization of concrete projects and measures represents the pillar of cross-border cooperation within EUREGIO EGRENSIS. What is it all about?

In terms of the projects themselves, most of them are presently being realized in the cultural, scientific, and educational spheres.

EUREGIO EGRENSIS attaches great importance to the realization of model projects from the "Trilateral Development Concept". Among others this includes the following projects:

- Establishment of a cross-border research and development company, i.e. the "EUREGIO EGRENSIS R&D Limited Liability Company" (already realized)

- Set-up of two centers for ecological and landscape orientated construction, as well as for historical construction. These centers strive to advise and inform on architectural styles typical for the region, ecologically compatible building materials, and energy-saving methods of building. In this context two essays exploring the realization possibilities are presently being prepared

- Intensification of the cooperation between spas and health resorts. A joint development and marketing concept is to be prepared. At different locations within EUREGIO EGRENSIS an appealing photo exhibition is presented to the public, complete with attractive impressions of these places

- Establishment of cross-border railway and passenger traffic, a project which has been acknowledged as a decentralized Expo 2000 project due to the Saxonian efforts

- Implementation of a cross-border qualification offensive, which will offer a qualification in trend-setting jobs to more than 600 unemployed persons

Representing a few important projects in the fields of business, transportation, infrastructure, and labor market, the following ideas deserve to be mentioned:

- a cross-border shopping guide, including information on cross-border shopping
- the Euroregional student exchange
- the cross-border landscape network
- the shaping of the cooperation with Finland, for instance by presenting a tapestry exposition, or by drawing up a report on the cooperation
- the financial support of cross-border cultural activities, such as the "Festival Middle Europe"
- the Euroregional youth summer camp
- the development and edition of 12 car theme-routes
- the set up and presentation of the exposition "Encounters along the Road"
- cross-border sports projects, such as EUREGIO EGRENSIS race, the cross-border cycling championships, or the cross-border glider championships
- the cross-border long-distance cycling trail
- cross-border congresses and conferences on regional topics and those concerning European politics

4. Prospects of cross-border cooperation

For the prospects of cross-border cooperation within EUREGIO EGRENSIS, mainly considering the forthcoming restructuring of the EU regional and structural policy, a growing regional political involvement, initiatives dealing with European politics, and an intensification of cross-border regional and project management are requested.

More and more often EUREGIO EGRENSIS is also being called upon to accept regional responsibilities, considering

- the forthcoming fundamental changes of the European structural funds
- the restructuring of the number, financial amount, and background of the EU joint initiatives' sponsorship
- the planned efficient integration of the CEE-states into the European Union (possibly already in 2004), and, interconnected, their declaration as areas of top priority sponsorship (first priority areas/Objective 1 region)

The possibility of taking part in the shaping of the EU joint initiative INTERREG III is therefore an important topic and concern of EUREGIO EGRENSIS. Clearly Euroregions, due to their competence concerning cross-border matters and European policy, are in an excellent position to take the lead in representing the opinions of business, administration, and citizens of borderland areas. The Euroregions in the Bavarian/ Austrian borderlands will probably be the only organizations to receive a special position. The European Commission is planning to grant a block allowance for the institutional promotion and the realization of smaller projects to the Euroregions in the Bavarian/Czech borderlands. The contracts would be signed directly between the Euroregions and the EU, with the Euroregions being directly called to account for the use of these funds by the EU. This step would represent another significant contribution to the invigoration of the Euroregions.

As for the theoretical shaping, the focus of attention will remain in the field of cross-border regional and project management, because it is almost exclusively the Euroregions which, due to their cross-border structure, can ideally meet the challenges involved.

Thus, EUREGIO EGRENSIS contributes significantly to an exchange of views, the search for identity, and the invigoration of creative environments in the Bavarian/Czech borderlands. It can already be seen how it will be the Euroregions which will play a vital role in the European expansion and unification process, especially on a regional and municipal level.

Cross-border Cooperation: Romania and Hungary

SIMONA PASCARIU

1. Background and general context

The changes and challenges which have taken place in the last decade or so in Eastern and Central Europe, together with the Western European perspective on the whole Europe on territory, demand an entirely new approach in the border areas, regarding the following crucial aspects:

- Market-oriented relations among the former "sister countries"
- Stability and sustainability
- European regionalization and European accessibility
- Selective permeability of the borders
- Compatibility with the CBC (cross-border cooperation) and Euroregions in the EU
- Competitiveness and attractiveness for potential foreign investors
- The pre-accession process towards EU membership
- Decentralization and democratization
- Ethnic minority rights/problems
- Balanced development at the regional level (NUTS II) in the national frame

Important documents like ESDP (Towards Balanced and Sustainable Development of the Territory of the EU), Potsdam, May 10/11, 1999 provide "Selected Programmes and Visions for Integrated Spatial Development" (pp. 77/79) as a basis for determining a strategy for the different regions within and adjacent to the EU. One of these programs is Phare, a program which "contains complementary approaches to the EU Community initiatives INTERREG II A and INTERREG II C and is therefore intended to support cross-border and transnational collaboration between EU Member States and non-Member States. Multisectorial projects are also promoted."

In this EU perspective, both Romania and Hungary are actors in the Central, Adriatic, Danubian and South Eastern European Space (CADSES).

In its turn, the VISION document has been elaborated on in the framework of the INTERREG II C project VISION PLANET. The initiating EU member countries were Austria, Germany and Italy, the participating non-EU member countries Bulgaria, Croatia, Czech Republic, Hungary, Poland, Romania, Slovakia, Slovenia and Yugoslavia. The VISION document, a draft was published shortly after the adoption of ESDP, actually consists of two major parts:

1. the "Policy Option Paper" contains the most important objectives and policy options of spatial planning cooperation and the recommendations for measures to be taken

2. the "Background Report" (to be finished in late 1999) contains the important findings of the common elaboration process and serves as a foundation and explanation for the objectives and measures described in the "Policy Option Paper"

Regarding the topic of this paper, it is important to mention that both Romania and Hungary are part of the CADSES area and different regional scenarios are working to achieve the fundamental objectives of the spatial development policy in the VISION-CADSES area, among which should be mentioned:

- *Balanced development and cohesion*: "Spatial development policy should contribute to a more balanced structure of the economy and society by strengthening economic, social and spatial cohesion and by supporting areas facing problems of underdevelopment or of especially severe structural change" (p. 7)

- The *balanced and sustainable spatial development,* being the relationship and interaction between the objectives. "Spatial sustainability has demographic, economic, social, environmental, natural and cultural aspects and dimensions and it means to establish equilibrium among these different aspects. It is especially important to define the requirements of sustainability in a period of critical transition which most of the countries of the VISION area are facing." (p. 10)

- And finally: "Trying to establish an adequate and delicate equilibrium in pursuing the different objectives is one of the tasks of regional policy and planning. There is no a priori ranking among objectives. The particular situation and point of time can decide the *actual priority ranking* to be followed. It is the "art of the trade" and the challenge regional policy and planning are confronted with." (POP, draft May, p. 11).

Regarding the regional policy development process, a law was adopted in December 1996 in Hungary, and in Romania in July 1998. Both countries are developing their specific regional bodies in order to set up working systems for regional competitive management.

According to the new Romanian law on Regional Development (151/15), one of the basic objectives of the regional development (art. 2.d.) is to "stimulate inter-regional, domestic, international and cross-border cooperation, Euroregions included, as well the participation of the development regions in the European structures and organizations promoting the institutional and the economic development of the former, with a view to achieving projects of common interest, according to the international agreements to which Romania is part".

The length of Romania's borders is 2,946 km (NATIONAL COMMISSION OF STATISTICS NCS 1998). It shares a common border with five countries:

- Hungary 445 km
- Yugoslavia 544 km
- Bulgaria 631 km
- Ukraine 635 km
- Moldova 692 km

A total of 19 counties (out of a total of 42 – including Bucharest – with a total population of almost 10 millions inhabitants) have border areas. The total surface of the border counties covers 119,855 km² (50.77% of Romania's total area).

Border counties and their surface in km²: Botoşani 4,986, Suceava 8,553, Maramureş 6,304, Satu Mare 4,418, Bihor 7,554, Arad 7,754, Timiş 8,697, Caraş-Severin 8,520, Mehedinţi 4,933, Dolj 7,414, Olt 5,498, Teleorman 5,790, Giurgiu 3,526, Călăraşi 5,088, Constanţa 7,071, Tulcea 8,499, Galaţi 4,466, Vaslui 5,318, Iaşi 5,476.

The significance of cross-border cooperation for the country is increasing and is being taken into consideration more and more both at national and regional levels.

This issue should also be seen in relation to the process of integration with the European Union and compatibility with the operation of the EU Structural Funds in the longer term.

2. Regional development process in Romania

2.1 The Romanian concept of regional development

The general reform being promoted by the Government of Romania includes regional development policy as a substantial component. The basic objectives of this policy are set out in art. 2 of Law 151/1998 and the first and most fundamental of these objectives is:

"... To reduce the existing regional disparities, in particular by stimulating well-balanced development, by accelerating recovery in those areas whose development has been lagging due to historical, geographical, economical, social and political circumstances, and to resist the emergence of new imbalances."

The Green Paper on Regional Development in Romania (accepted by the Romanian Government in 1997) pointed out that:

"Disparities in the level of development of different regions result from their initial endowments of natural and human resources and the patterns of change (economic, technological, demographic, social, political and cultural) that have shaped their development throughout history."

Market forces tend to favor the enlargement of existing disparities. Industrial centers or service areas tend to be more developed whilst marginal areas with an agricultural profile or low communication facilities become more marginal.

Such tendencies can result not only in the relative impoverishment of specific regions but also in the general level of performance of the national economy being lower than it would be if economic activity were distributed more evenly across the national territory.

The broad process of economic and administrative decentralization is also reflected in the law where another explicitly stated objective is to co-ordinate the sectoral policies of the government with local and regional initiatives and resources "with a view to attaining the sustainable economic, social and cultural development" of the regions.

These processes of stimulating regional activities, coordinating them with the policies of the central government (while ensuring that national sectoral policies reflect regional needs) and promoting inter-regional cooperation represent a concerted effort by the Romanian Government to meet the particular needs of Romania and all of its regions. However, they are also all placed explicitly by the Law on Regional Development in the context of Romania's application for EU membership in general and the preparatory process of developing appropriate institutional structures and capacities in relation to EU regional policies in particular.

As it was stated by the Green Paper:

"In order to take on the obligations of the EU membership, an applicant state must achieve certain pre-accession objectives with respect to socio-economic development, amongst which the rectification of economic imbalance between the different regions of the country is a high priority."

2.2 Policy concerns and the approach chosen

Romania is sub-divided into 42 counties (*judeţs*) including Bucharest for administrative purposes and to allow for more democratic government. However the counties do not cover large enough areas to be effective for the purposes of designing and implementing regional development policy. It was therefore proposed in the Green Paper that groups of counties with complementary socio-economic profiles should be encouraged to combine into development regions on a voluntary basis. These **Development Regions** would be large enough to both allow efficient use of resources and provide meaningful context for the elaboration and implementation of the regional strategies. They would also be appropriate for the collection and analysis of socio-economic data.

The Green Paper went on to propose that "priority areas" should be specified within the development regions. These would be groupings of contiguous communes, cities or counties with similar significant regional development problems. The Green Paper identified sixteen different priority areas in Romania, each containing one or more of four types of development problems:

- High levels of poverty
- Industrial decline
- High level of pollution
- Soil degradation

While many of these priority areas fall completely within single development areas, others do not. The manner in which the approach to priority areas was to be articulated in the development region structure was not specified in the Green Paper.

2.3 Institutional framework

The territory of Romania is divided into 8 Development Regions (see map) – representing areas corresponding to a group of counties, based upon an agreement signed by the representatives of the county councils, as follows:

Development Region	Counties / Judeţs component of the region:
Northeast	Bacău, Botoşani, Iaşi, Suceava, Vaslui
Southeast	Brăila, Buzau, Constanţa, Galaţi, Tulcea, Vrancea
South – Muntenia	Argeş, Călăraşi, Dâmboviţa, Giurgiu, Ialomiţa, Prahova, Teleorman
Southwest – Oltenia	Dolj, Gorj, Mehedinţi, Olt, Vâlcea
West – Romania	Arad, Caraş-Severin, Hunedoara, Timiş
Northwest	Bihor, Bistriţa-Năsăud, Cluj, Maramureş, Sălaj, Satu Mare
Centre	Alba, Braşov, Covasna, Harghita, Mureş, Sibiu
Bucureşti – Ilfov	Bucureşti, Ilfov

Among these regions only the Center and Bucureşti-Ilfov are not border regions.

The population of the 8 regions and a regional hierarchy based on the population figure (NCS, Romanian Statistical Yearbook) was, in 1996:

Regions	Population 1996	% of the total
1. West Romania	2,076,702	9.2
2. Bucureşti – Ilfov	2,314,754	10.2
3. South West – Oltenia	2,429,320	10.7
4. Centre	2,666,288	11.8
5. Northwest	2,872,850	12.8
6. Southeast	2,948,750	13.0
7. South – Muntenia	3,510,799	15.5
8. Northeast	3,788,157	16.8
Total	**22,607,620**	**100.0**

For these regions the following was set up:

- **Decision-making bodies**
    - A Regional Development Board is set up each development region, made up of the representatives of the county and local authorities in each component county
    - The National Board for Regional Development is set up at the national level, composed of representatives from the government and from the development regions in equal numbers, chaired by the Prime Minister

- **Executive bodies**
  - *A Regional Development Agency is to be established in each region,* as a non-governmental body and a legal entity
  - *The National Agency for Regional Development* is established at the national level, as a specialized body of the central public administration, reporting to the Government

- **Financial Instruments**
  - A Regional Development Fund is set up in each development region, managed by the Regional Development Agency
  - The National Fund for Regional Development is set up at the national level, managed by the National Agency for Regional Development

2.4 The legal and institutional provisions

Starting with the second half of 1998 a series of legislative steps were taken to establish the basis for the design and delivery of regional policy in Romania along the lines described above

- Law No. 151/1998 concerning regional development in Romania
- Government Decision No. 634/1998, on approval of the Methodological Norms for implementation of Law No. 151/1998
- Government Decision No. 979/1998, for the designation of the representatives from the Government in the National Board for Regional Development
- Government Decision No. 979/1998, for the organization and operation of the National Agency for Regional Development
- Law No. 20/1999, for the approval of the Government Emergency Ordinance No. 24/1998 concerning the Less Favored Areas

In terms of institutional establishment, the National Agency for Regional Development, all eight Regional Boards and Agencies and the National Board for Regional Development were established by the end of March 1999. The National Agency and all of the Regional Agencies are at present in the process of appointing personnel.

3. Short presentation of the regional characteristics of the region bordering Hungary

Since 1994, the Phare Program has provided support to facilitate cross-border co-operation (CBC) along the borders of Central and Eastern European countries with adjacent regions in the EU Member States. The continuation of the Phare CBC Program beyond 1994 to 1999 in order to coincide with the INTERREG II A initiative has been supported by the countries of Central and Eastern Europe and by the European Commission which regards cross-border cooperation as an important tool for the pre-accession strategy of both Romania and Hungary into the European Union. In addition, the European Council at its Essen summit supported the continuation of the Phare CBC program in December 1994.

The 1996 CBC program includes an allocation to support activities which promote cross-border cooperation on the border between Hungary and Romania. Projects selected for funding in the framework of the Romanian program include infrastructure projects as well as the preparation of a Regional Development Strategy for the eligible border region which consists of the four counties of (from south to north) Timişoara, Arad, Bihor and Satu-Mare. The Hungarian counterpart program also includes, inter alia, the preparation of a "Regional Development Concept" for the border counties concerned. These are the counties of Békés, Csongrád, Hajdú-Bihar and Szabolcs-Szatmár-Bereg.

The Romanian counties on the border with Hungary, have been parts of distinct historic provinces:

- Banat (the Timiş county and some areas of the Arad county)
- Crişana (some areas of the Arad county and the Bihor county)
- Maramureş (the Satu-Mare county)

For social, economic and other reasons, the cross-border region is a coherent economic and geographic area. A considerable amount of inter-regional cooperation between individual counties or groups of counties already exists, although there is an equally strong element of competition.

Although the four counties belong to the more prosperous ones in Romania, there are a number of issues which affect economic development. In parts of the border region (for example Timiş county) agriculture retains an important share of GDP and the production system is in need of modernization. The privatization process is underway and traditional industries are in need of restructuring. Although small and medium sized enterprises are gradually emerging, this process needs to be supported. Economic restructuring has led to a rise in unemployment in all four counties which is comparatively low in Timiş (3.8%) but rising in the northern part of the border region, (e.g. 6.2% in Satu Mare) which is generally less developed. The border region has relatively poor infrastructure and communications (e.g. rail and road network) but is well placed within a broader European and Central European context. Hungarian minorities have a strong presence in the border region.

A general presentation of the Romanian Border Regions is given in Annex A, comprising the main characteristics for all these NUTS II areas. But the Romanian CBC area with Hungary is part of two development regions as follows:

- Arad and Timiş in the Development Region 5 West
- Bihor and Satu Mare in the Development Region 6 North West

The same "*decoupage*" is present in the Hungarian CBC area with Romania (Csongrád and Békés are in one Development Region and Hajdú-Bihar and Szabolcz-Szatmár-Bereg in another).

To ensure a proper approach and good subsequent development of the CBC process at the Romanian/Hungarian border, the liaisons with and the linkages among these four RDA's should be, together with the county decision-making level, the key stakeholders, owners and promoters of the common strategy (see Chapter 4).

In order to understand the regional priorities and strategy objectives for CBC, it is necessary to draw attention to some socio-geo-economic characteristics of this Romanian Region bordering Hungary:

- the length of the border is 445 km, having a general north-east – south-west orientation. This length covers the entire western border of Satu Mare, Bihor and Arad counties, and some tens of km's in Timiş county
- the osmosis of the border, measured through the national, transnational and trans-regional flows of people and goods tends to be more and more related to the cooperation at the regional, county and local levels
- the political function of the border was not so strong between 1950 – 1990, because both states had a communist, socialist orientation, and after 1990 were in a transition process. However, the recent developments at the continental level have tended to maximize the divisive function of the frontier (This has to do with Hungary's membership in NATO and its starting of the pre-accession process into the EU, which might lead to a selective permeability in the border area)
- a major characteristic of the physical geography is the general orientation of the hydrographic basin towards Hungary (generating common problems regarding water management and the prevention of floods)
- the general conditions of the environment have a relatively good stability with some fragility areas
- due to the industrialization process in the 70's, the depopulation in the rural area (mostly in the mountains and hilly areas) and the pre-existing historical conditions, there are four poles of economic growth in this region where 90% of the industrial production and some 85% of the specialized services (health, culture, higher education) are concentrated
- the area in question is one of the most "mixed" areas in the country, with Romanians, Serbs, Germans, Croats, Ukrainians and other nationalities living together here. Before 1970, on the Timiş county territory the German-speaking population made up the majority and nowadays, in the Satu Mare county the Hungarian population is over 35%. This is also the region with the highest number of mixed marriages in Romania
- preserving the identity of the population in their traditional environment within the frame of modern life constitutes one of the main practical challenges for the region. The lack of adequate strategies, negligence, vandalism and other actions, inappropriate forms of tourism or simply idleness could endanger forever all of the heritage we are so proud of

- the geographical position of the urban poles, the economic environment and the cultural behavior of the population determine the attractiveness of the foreign investments toward these centers. It should be mentioned that the investments are made in diverse sectors and fields of activity

- the four main cities (Arad, Oradea, Timişoara and Satu Mare) are located on the main transport corridors (road and rail) between Romania and Hungary. However, Timişoara has built a strong relation with Western Europe via Belgrade in the last 3 – 4 decades, less through Hungary, but those trans-border relations were increasing significant during the last years.

The cross-border program – a strategic perspective

Spatial planning and regional development of some border areas have been taken into account since the 50's. It was hypothesized and then proved by tangible results that cross-border cooperation creates "development corridors" which generate relations and interrelations of exchange and economic development, facilitate flows of people, goods, information and culture, bringing added value and sustainability.

- The Phare CBC Romania-Hungary 1996 Program is a pilot program among two Phare countries, and represents the willingness of the interested parties to create such "development corridors" in the Hungarian-Romanian border area in a strategic perspective (aimed at):

- involving the regional and local authorities as key players in the development policy

- achieving the regional objectives (due to and promoted by these key players) through their cooperation with each other in line with the "bottom-up" approach

- setting up common organizations, structures and networks and elaborating cross-border spatial development strategies

- providing in future a common basis for a number of cross-border operational programs, linking different projects in key considerated areas (i.e. transport, environment, economic development, urban and rural issues)

The chosen approach in this strategy was the identification of the regional objectives able to solve the needs and priorities at the county level and on this basis the elaboration of a Strategy Action Plan, including specific measures, programs and projects.

The Regional Study project and main issues

The Regional Study project comprises a systematic approach to the production of a comprehensive strategy for the cross-border region. The importance of the strategy should be seen in terms of both a process, which will enhance the capacity of the region in terms of regional development, and a final output comprising a document which will identify priorities and measures for the development of the border region.

The Regional Study will build the regional strategy on the basis of consolidating strategies, which are to be developed for each of the Romanian counties involved. The final document will provide a strategy for the development of the cross-border region on both sides of the Romanian and Hungarian border.

All counties have developed cross-border activities with Hungarian partners in different sectors. Examples are cooperation activities between businesses, universities and other actors. The presence of Hungarian/Romanian minorities on either side of the border has led to various cross-border activities in the cultural sphere. In some cases this has led to the signing of co-operation protocols between neighboring counties, e.g. Arad, Timiş / Békés, Csongrád. Despite these efforts, there exists no regular broader forum for joint discussion and planning of the potential of the border region as a whole and across several sectors.

On the Hungarian side, the 1996 *Act on Regional Development and Physical Planning* states the regional development is to be coordinated at the level of the counties. The Act also introduces the concept of *regions* as a policy element for planning and development purposes, and for the financial development of projects that go beyond the concerns of one individual county. County Development Councils have been set up in the four counties participating in the project and were actively involved in program preparation and project selection. County Development Strategies in accordance with the Hungarian Regional Development Concept have been developed in some of these counties. The Hungarian counterpart project started this April (one year later than the Romanian one).

Since the start of this process (considered as such and not a project having a beginning and an end), a number of significant aspects could be underlined, in order to identify the strategic priorities, the crucial objectives, the specific policies and the key actors and networks able to put in place a (functioning) system of cross-border economic development in the region:

4.1.1 Local administration

As was the case in most Central and East European Countries, in Romania, the decentralization also meant in most cases the transfer of responsibilities toward the lower levels of the system. However, the legislative framework is still incomplete and often the missing part is the democratic mechanism for the management of public affairs (based on the nearest territoriality concept and the direct contact between the elected officials and the inhabitants).

As a general consequence, the major problem in the field is the establishment of an adequate policymaking capacity at local and regional level.

In Romania (in the border region too) there is at present still the lack of an efficient management and the existence of pressures, tensions related to the reform.

4.1.2 Raising awareness and dialogue

During the start of this Phare CBC Regional Study project (April 1998) everyone of its work-phases were preceded by several working meetings in each of the four involved Romanian counties: Timiş, Arad, Bihor and Satu Mare. These meetings, including the workshops and counties conferences, were meant to bring together in broader forums or working groups the key actors (decision-makers, business-persons, specialists, managers, media, a.s.o.), to discuss and share their views regarding the topic.

It was clear even from the very beginning that step by step the issue was understood, leading to the crystallization of some important regional objectives and priorities. However, another observation is that it is very difficult to expand a strategic perspective beyond the county limits. Even if, the cross-border cooperation with the Hungarian's is welcome, the acceptance of a regional priority in the other three counties is very difficult. The most successful aspect related to the awareness raising and the dialogue is the real involvement and perspectives opened by this diverse participation.

4.1.3 Tradition and modernity

Sixty or seventy years ago, a fair in the Romanian-Hungarian border region in Timiş county area, naturally brought farmers and other people together. They came from neighboring areas and had different ethnic backgrounds (Germans, Hungarians, Romanians, Serbs, Croats, Gypsies). Administrative national borders did not hamper this event.

Then, for at least fifty years, this kind of coming together was forbidden. Today, the network of "links" should be rebuilt on the basis of this common tradition and history. What is different however is that the newly emerging idea of possibilities offered by the new Age of Information and new technologies should be implemented as well in order to attract investments and a young, well-qualified labor force into the region.

4.1.4 Projects, projects, projects

The CBC process is being and will continue to be supported by specific projects in the fields and sectors identified by the strategy as priorities (e.g. infrastructure, environment, human resources, culture, SMEs, networking, etc.). In order to attract these funds for development, the region will face a strong competition between Romania and Hungary, but among the Romanian and Hungarian counties as well.

The crucial issues for proposal and selection of projects should take into consideration some criteria such as:

- CBC impact or mirrored effect
- facilities and local/regional support
- management at local/regional level
- costs
- number of people affected
- effectiveness and efficiency
- use of local/regional resources
- partnership

The Regional Study will propose a set of criteria (in accordance with the Hungarian partners) for the use of the projects included in the Small Projects Funds (1999), which received a lump sum of 500,000 €. It will also prepare the frame for all the projects starting in 2000. One important aspect is that a Joint Coordinating Committee will be involved in the selection process.

4.1.5 SMEs and NGOs

It is obvious in the restructuring of the society (in itself) and the regional economy that both SMEs and NGOs represent key factors for the development. The potential dynamism, flexibility and (a relative) independence of this kind of organization will facilitate the process of CBC and help it to spread quickly and gain better understanding in the region.

Another important element is represented by the diversity of sectors covered: from agriculture and tourism, to industry and culture.

4.1.6 Region/sub-regions/counties?

As mentioned before, the four Romanian counties involved are parts of two development regions:

- Arad and Timiş in the West Development Region
- Bihor and Satu Mare in the Northwest Development Region

The same situation occurs in the Hungarian part of the CBC Romainian/Hungarian region. It will be of crucial importance to identify specific priorities at these different levels:

- between 2 counties (one Romanian and one Hungarian)
- between 2 sub-regions (2 Romanian and 2 Hungarian counties)
- between the Romanian and the Hungarian border regions (4 counties each)
- in all CBC regions (8 counties)

A correct distribution and selection of these priorities will be one of the key success factor for the entire process of cooperation and development.

4.1.7 Interface

This issue should be covered in the following perspectives, activities:

- providing technical assistance for the SWOT analyses, diagnoses and elaboration of the joint CBC strategy
- enabling and creating a frame for a dialogue between the interested actors
- getting involved in the cooperation process, as direct partner for both Romanian and Hungarian local and regional authorities
- providing know-how, best practices and support to the regional beneficiaries
- generating a framework for debates for the target groups of the CBC process and for the potential financing organizations
- becoming actively involved as partners in the process

4.1.8 CBC institutionalization

One of the tasks of the Regional Study is the proposal of a joint Romainian/Hungarian structure able to carry out the CBC process in the region. Problems like different legislation systems and financing can be overcome by setting up – in an inception phrase – an institution having as its major task the management of a commonly agreed upon problem. However, this issue should be discussed with Hungarian partners thoroughly and linked to existing organizations dealing with the cross-border issues in the region.

4.1.9 Synergy

Another crucial element of the CBC process is the creation of synergy of activities, projects and programs included, in order to avoid overlapping. A key related issue is to co-ordinate CBC activities in the frame of different organizations and movements, regions and CBC institutions (e.g. the Eurocarpathian Region, Danube Mureş Criş Euroregion, Romainian/Hungarian CBC Region, the two RDAs, a.s.o.)

4.1.10 Partnership and priorities

In the end, the most important challenge is the capacity of building and the creation of a real partnership in the Romanian/Hungarian region. More and more (and the potential and existing conflict areas show this), the partnership is the most important frame for every positive development.

The Romanian-Hungarian region has a tremendous potential – natural and human resources, a strategic location, common traditions and history, ... Priorities for intervention should be identified on the basis of partnership if we want this potential to be sustainable.

Some mistakes are inevitable. But even so, a partnership approach is simply the best way to go.

4.2 The partnership with Hungarians – perspectives/institution building

Since the start of the Romanian Regional Study it was clear that:

- only with the Hungarian participation can this project be achieved in a proper way
- the Hungarians have better consolidated local (county) strategies and have more experience both at the local level and in CBC (i.e. The Complex Regional Development Concept of the Western Cross-Border Region of Hungary, at Hungarian/ Austrian border)
- this CBC project should represent the start of an on-going cooperation process, and after the Phare project ends it should be carried on by local and regional structures/actors

Between April 1998 (Romanian project starting date) and April 1999 (the Hungarian one), a number of initiatives and actions took place in the border region (both in Romania and Hungary) in order to improve and to increase the awareness of the stakeholders regarding the CBC process and opportunities. These actions were made by inviting Hungarian actors involved in the regional and local development to participate at the CBC working meeting in the four Romanian counties, involving Hungarian experts and consultants to facilitate the SWOT analysis and setting-up objectives at the county level for Arad, Bihor, Satu Mare and Timiş and constantly informing the Regional Offices in Arad (set up for the Romanian border) and in Bekecsaba (set up for the Hungarian border) about any progress made in the project's implementation.

After the Hungarian mirrored project started, a working meeting took place in Budapest and it was agreed that:

- there will be equal Hungarian/Romanian participation at the partner workshops, training courses and other activities
- there will be common selection criteria (technical and financial) for project selection in the border area
- there will be special meetings for the elaboration of CBC projects on the basis of joint training and common objectives/priorities
- the Joint Strategy will have a common statement for the whole CBC region, and special provision for the Romanian and Hungarians areas
- the main fields of cooperation focused on: economic development, environment and water management, infrastructure, human resources, cultural issues
- the involvement of respective RDAs is crucial and CBC objectives should be promoted by them in accordance with the regional perspectives and national sectoral policies
- the CBC Institution building should be common and based on existing possibilities (see Annex B).

5. Some conclusions

Now, one year after this Regional Study project started, it is clear that many doors have been opened to the development of this trans-border region at the national, regional and local levels. All the major actors involved in this process agree to participate and to take their respective responsibilities. However, it also clear that despite this general acceptance, there are a number of major risks which can jeopardize it. Some of these risks are:

- The region will not be able to constitute a single, strong voice
- The counties involved will not understand how to cooperate in the process
- The RDAs involved will not include the CBC strategy concept in their own concept
- The funds allocated for the specific projects can be stopped
- The permeability of the border could be selective, after Hungary's accession into the EU structures
- The immediate results not be apparent (for quite some time)

If one were to compare the program of regionalization of the country to a fitness program, the CBC program might constitute a body-building exercise. However, certain specific threats have been identified as well:

From a Romanian perspective, the "dangers" have to do with the idea that the Hungarian counties will derive greater benefits from the cooperation than the Romanian. This are fears that this whole thing is nothing, a so-called preparation of the region to become Hungarian territory in the future. For the Hungarians, on the other hand, the "dangers" have to do with the fact that there is a tendency to view the border area from the national development level. In fact, the four Romanian and four Hungarian border counties are more similar in terms of figures than the national averages. This could reduce the interest of potential investors in cross-border projects(programs. A common danger is the overlapping of different efforts, with the direct effect of diluting and delaying the cross-border process and the continuation of the chaotic exchanges and flows.

What are the solutions?

- Improving communication (WEB Observatories), common TV & Radio broadcasting, journals and leaflets with CBC opportunities and activities/events, in order to create a stronger regional trans-border identity

- Shortening the distance by facilitating the access to information and institutions at local/regional level

- Searching for investors, donors and co-finance also from other sources than Phare CBC on the basis of the common strategy (common priorities, interests and benefits), by undertaking joint actions and measures and improving the region marketing activity.

Finally, it has to be mentioned that the CBC strategic regional approach for the Romanian/Hungarian border area was recently adopted for the Romanian/Bulgarian border and in spring 1999 the Joint Programming was signed for the next three years between these two countries.

Annex A

Figure 1 Development Regions in Romania

6. Short profiles of the Romanian border regions

Of the eight Romanian development regions, six are border regions. These regions do not represent administrative-territory units, as the first administrative division after the whole national territory is the county (*judeţs*).

6.1 Northeast Development Region

The region covering the north-eastern corner of the country includes 6 counties: **Botoşani, Bacău, Iaşi, Suceava, Neamţ and Vaslui**. Traditionally, this region is part of the old historical region of Moldova. The county of Suceava is known as part of a smaller historical region, Bucovina (the Beech-tree Country). The region appears one of the poorest – if not the poorest – in Romania, facing a large range of problems, from high unemployment to environmental issues. A study carried out by the World Bank in 1977 (Romania, Poverty and Social Policy, Report no. 16462 – RO, World Bank, HRS Operation Division, Country Department I, Europe and Central Asia Region, April 1997) indicates that there are over 1.1 million people in these 6 counties living below the poverty threshold, which is close to $1/4^{th}$ of the total population of Romania.

The region can be seen as the main center of origin for the mass emmigration to other counties. However, within the region, Iaşi and, to a certain extent, Bacău are the main centers of attraction. The industrial structure (including textile sector, chemistry and metallic products) of the Northeast Region involves only 25% of the occupied population (against 42% in agriculture), and seems to be very fragile for the free market economy due to its low productivity and economic efficiency.

As consequence, the region is less able to cope with the new economic conditions, the reform process and the free competition. Moreover, the population of the region (comprised of 98% Romanians against the national mean 89.4%) is characterized more by a certain conservative feeling than by openness to change and modernization.

The border neighbors, Ukraine and the Republic of Moldova (both former USSR) are connected to the region by road and rail lines, but there are strong traditional and historical links still evident.

6.2 Southeast Development Region

This region has a very irregular form and includes 6 counties: **Buzău, Brăila, Constața, Galați, Tulcea, Vrancea**. It covers a large area from the mountains in the west to the Black Sea Coast to the east.

The region is composed of different historical areas including part of Moldova (to the north), Muntenia (to the south) and Dobrogea (to the east). It is probably the most heterogeneous region among the eight. It may also be described as a composition of several specific areas: the western side is closer to the mountainous and hilly areas (especially Vrancea county) with a medium low level of urbanization, Brăila is a typical traditional agricultural area and Dobrogea is famous for its tourist attractions – the Danube Delta and the Black Sea Coast. There are two major agglomerations, Galați, well known as the metallurgic center of the country and Constanța, the maritime gate of Romania and one of the biggest harbors on the Black Sea.

The region appears to be a medium-developed region according to most of the indicators. It is a region which is very much based on a few highly-developed areas and on a few industrial branches located in some gigantic complexes. As a consequence, the region faces high discrepancies between the urban agglomeration and the much broader rural zones. Practically, the region has to support and is developing around the double polarity of the Constanța and Brăila-Galați areas.

Also, the weak connection of Dobrogea to the rest of the country and to foreign neighbors, together with its environmental issues represent the critical problem areas facing the region.

In the end, the region as a whole has a medium low-level of participation rate (268/1000), a rate of uncmployment (11%) slightly higher than the national average and a dynamic participation 1995/1990 roughly equivalent to the national mean.

6.3 South Development Region – Muntenia

This region is made up of a cluster of seven counties totalling 34,400 km^2. Five of them – **Giurgiu, Călărași, Ialomița, Prahova and Dâmbovița** are direct neighbors to the capital city of București and two others – **Argeș and Teleorman** – even they do not border it directly are close to it.

The whole South Region is included into the historical region of Muntenia. (Only two counties in Muntenia – Brăila and Buzău – are outside of this development region.)

Teleorman, Giurgiu, Călăraşi and Ialomiţa are located in the Central Romanian Plain and are bordered by the Danube and Bulgaria.

The South Region is clearly divided into two sub-regions. The northern part (Argeş, Dâmboviţa and Prahova) is a rich area (oil and coal industry, big potential for tourism). The southern part (Teleorman, Ialomiţa, Giurgiu and Călăraş) is predominantly agricultural and strongly affected by the Bucureşti area.

In spite of this strong contrast in terms of development, the two sub-regions could function as a development or project region. Their geographic location and the communication network are the key factors favoring this potential for regional development.

The potential for cooperation and common actions of development is especially high for the plain poor communes which are located at the border.

The region has the largest disparities in terms of standard of living, participation rate, communication infrastructure and human capital. These disparities could be reduced to a large degree by fostering local cooperation between south agriculture and north industry, by improving communication infrastructure, by developing private agriculture.

6.4 Southwest Development Region – Oltenia

This region is formed by all five counties in the historical region of Oltenia: **Dolj, Gorj, Mehedinţi, Olt and Vâlcea**. It is situated between the Carpathian mountains and Danube in the southwestern part of the country. Former Yugoslavia and Bulgaria are its neighbors to the south. Due to its location and natural resources, conditions are favorable for a high potential of development of this region.

The region could be greatly affected by the development of transport infrastructure, due to its geographical potential. That's why the option for a future bridge over the Danube will have huge implications on the future development of the entire South Region.

For a long period, this region was a reservoir of labor for other regions (mostly Bucureşti and Banat areas). Since so many people have left the region, the region has a high degree of population aging, especially in its southwest part and in isolated rural areas. A demographic revival of the central part of the region started three decades ago when lignite was first mined and some of the country's largest hydro-energetic plants were constructed.

Considering the resources of the region, its economy might be defined by its rural character in large expanses. An important trait of the region as a whole is the energetic dominance of the economy, defined on the one hand by the exploitation of coal and oil resources, and on the other hand, by the presence of the biggest hydro-electrical plants in the country.

Complex and complicated problems could be the ones of reintegration in the economic circuit of spaces. Again, the favorable geographical position, the real possibilities of cross-border cooperation, and also the agricultural resources of this region can constitute advantages in the economic revitalization process, overcome the crisis period caused by restructuring of economic activities.

6.5 Development Regions West and Northwest

Due to their importance for the topic, these two development regions will be analyzed in a special chapter.

6.6 West-Romania Development Region

The West Region of Romania, formed by the association of four counties: **Arad, Timiş, Hunedoara and Caraş-Severin**, is based on a strong cultural identity with obvious influences from its German-speaking population and on complementary resources. The region's geographical position sets it apart and moreover, provides ample opportunities for cross-border cooperation.

Highlands and lowlands – with the whole range of variegated and specific elements almost equally divided – dominate the natural background. There are few hills, so that the mountain often ends at the plain. The relatively sudden transition from one natural unit to the other, usually divided by a large intermediary area, proves to be an asset for communication and cooperation of distinct zones that have complementary resources.

The total **population** of the West Region numbers 2.2 million people. Densities of about 67 inhabitants per km^2, place it far behind other macro-regions of Romania. All four counties in this region are below the national average of 96 inhabitants per km^2 in terms of population density: Timiş (81 inhabitants per km^2), Hunedoara (75 inhabitants per km^2), Arad (67 inhabitants per km^2), and Caraş-Severin (46 inhabitants per km^2). Looking at the geographical conditions of these counties, it seems unrealistic to judge them by the population density criterion. Paradoxically, Hunedoara has a lower potential for settlement development (over 80% mountains, 20% high mountain zone; 55% woodland and alpine pastureland), yet it stays ahead of Arad *judeţ*. The fact is that Hunedoara has massive concentrations of population in depressions and valley corridors, making it one of the most highly urbanized counties in Romania.

The main demographic indicators are notably influenced by the one-child family pattern customary in Banat, which leads to a negative overall natural increase rate. However, demographic behavior has been optimized by the influx of a young labor force coming from other regions, especially from the northeast, where the large-family pattern is the rule. Hunedoara *judeţ*, dominated by the mining sector, improved its natural demographic indicators in the way shown above and also by absorbing many newcomers from the coal basin of Petroşani (the Jiu Valley) in particular.

The **settlement system** has 1,338 villages grouped into 269 communes, 36 towns of which only two have over 100,000 inhabitants, and notable density disparities between Banat proper and Hunedoara *judeţ* attached to the region. In Hunedoara, village density is 65 inhabitants per 1,000 km², while the other three counties tally nearly half that percentage (Caraş-Severin – 34; Arad – 36; Timiş – 37). The same goes for the average number of villages per commune: from 8 in Hunedoara to 4.1 in Arad, and 4.2 in Timiş and Caraş-Severin each. Hence, there are distinct problems of infrastructure and ways of gaining access to it.

Settlements in the plain are usually large-sized, while in the mountains they are small and medium-sized. These disparities are reinforced at *judeţ* level. With its 661 inhabitants per village Caraş-Severin is transitional from Hunedoara (309 inhabitants per village) to Arad and Timiş counties (914 and 1,006 inhabitants per village, respectively). Although the living standard in the region's countryside is fairly high, nevertheless depopulation is a reality. Before 1989, it was the attraction of the city, after that date it was the mass migration of the German-speaking people. However, a few plain villages, with a population of over 10,000 inhabitants (Pecica - 12,000; Sântana - 13,000) are among the largest in Romania.

The urban system has a fairly good structure at the upper ranks of the hierarchy, but is very disproportionate in the territory. Prominent is Timişoara City with nearly 350,000 inhabitants, followed by Arad (approx. 200,000) and Reşiţa with a population of 100,000. Although there are lots of towns (and their number seems to be sufficient) with a population of 20,000 – 100,000 they are spread out very unevenly. Out of the eleven towns in this group, eight are in Hunedoara *judeţ* only. Disproportion is particularly striking in Arad *judeţ,* where the 15/1 ratio between the size of the capital and the second-ranking town is suggestive.

Unlike Hunedoara, where small towns represent 38% of the total, this urban category is very numerous in Arad (86%), Timiş (71%) and Caraş-Severin even (62%).

The **economy** is distinctively different, but complementary. The fact that there is a certain symmetry of dominant economies is due to a specialized industry, based on almost similar subsoil resources. Looking at the similarity of the economy of Caraş-Severin and Hunedoara counties on the one hand, and of Arad and Timiş on the other, the idea emerged of establishing a joint cooperation and using their complementary resources.

In Caraş-Severin and Hunedoara there is coke, ferrous and non-ferrous ores, so extractive and metallurgical industries developed in both counties. Despite a two-hundred-year tradition, today they are being restructured. The large forest stock, only partially put to use, is another important resource. Part of the wood is processed in the big manufacturing units of Caransebeş, or in the small and medium-large enterprises of either *judeţs*. Some of it goes to the big processing units in Arad and Timiş. The very diverse mountainous landscapes, the host of natural tourist sites, the opportunities for practicing various sports, and the recreational advantages of a highland environment represent an important economic asset that has good prospects of future development.

The economy of Arad and Timiş counties is far more complex. There is a wider range of processing industries, including also agricultural products. The two prominent cities – Timişoara and Arad, have a wide-ranging industrial profile (machine-building, light industry and chemical industries in the main). Agriculture is an efficient sector with highly productive lands, and a lively animal-breeding sector. The related industries which process agricultural products have good prospects for development. The two counties have a nation-wide fame for swine herding in particular, with very high pork meat productions and processing capacities.

Major **transportation network** is represented by two transnational corridors: the national highways (E15A and E94), and two electric railways that link Romania to Central and Western Europe. The traffic is highest through the Mureş Corridor, which is also a transcontinental transit route used especially by trailers from Central and Western Europe heading to the southeast of the Continent and the Near East.

The **environment** is deteriorated in places by the high polluting industries. Frequently located in depressions or valley corridors, they have detrimental effects on the near-by human agglomerations. Highest pollution levels are registered in Petroşani Basin, where beside industrial activities there is a large household consumption of coal; in Hunedoara-Deva (from the sideurgical works in Hunedoara, the thermo-electrical power station at Mintia, the building material manufacturing unit at Chişcădaga); in the depression of Reşiţa (center of the siderurgical industry). In addition, there is surface pollution from chemical fertilizers and from the large animal farms located in the Timiş and in the Mureş Plains.

6.7 Conclusion

The West Region is one of the best-developed territories in Romania. It is a fairly complex multicultural space that has lots of varied natural resources and a favorable geographical position for cross-border cooperation. There is a marked distinction between the lowland and the highland counties, the former have a complex economic structure, with concentrations of population in one large city, and a higher living standard. The economy of the latter is focused on mining and metallurgy, and on associated and complementary branches.

The lowland countryside has been revitalized by a new Land Law that provides for the reinstatement of private property in agriculture. This helped farmers increase their revenues, develop local services and intensify the village/town relationship. As the sizeable urban industry in Timiş and Arad counties undergoes restructuring, the ratio of commuters dropped to 1/7, which means people are returning to work in their places of origin, where the development of small and medium-large manufacturers absorbed many of those who laid off.

The restructuring of the mining and metallurgical sectors in Hunedoara and Caraş-Severin counties has a significant impact on each settlement, because there are very few chances for people to find a job at local level. Many requested to be laid off so they could go back to where they had come from. However, this drain of the young labor force may create serious long-term development problems in these counties.

The Regional Development Agency of West Romania Region was set up in Timiş county, in Timişoara. It is very important to mention that, for the moment this is the only region which has any experience related to strategic development. On the basis of each county development agency (ADAR-Arad, ADETIM-Timiş, ADECS-Caraş Severin and ADEH-Hunedoara) supported by each County Council and North Rhein Westfalia, a common development strategy was issued in 1998, elaborating objectives and priorities for the region and outlining measures and actions.

6.8 Northwest Development Region

The Northwest Region includes 6 counties from the northwestern part of Romania: **Maramureş, Sălaj, Cluj, Bistriţa-Năsăud, Bihor and Satu-Mare**. These counties are interrelated in terms of natural resources and economic activities. The landscape of the Northwest Region is dominated by hills and low mountains; there are, as well, a few plains.

The total area of the Northwest Region is 34,000 km^2, and is characterized by a large variety of **natural conditions**. In the northeast (the north part of the Oriental Carpatian Mountains) and the southeast (the north of the Apuseni Mountains) there is a mountain area with mineral resources, forests and agriculture (in special pastures, meadows and livestock). Between the two mountainous areas there is an important hilly area, crossed by the Someş River and its affluent. In the western part there are the Someş and Criş plains which are low plains with a dominant agriculture profile.

The region **is highly populated**, owing to a favorable living potential; one important characteristic to be mentioned is the relative uniform diffusion of the localities. From a demographic viewpoint the negative natural increase rate is noticed (Bihor and Cluj have the lowest values: -3.5% and -3.2%). In Maramureş county and in Bistriţa-Năsăud the situation is different: there are positive natural increase rates due to the fact that in these areas the dominant family pattern is a family with many children.

The **settlement system** comprises 1,500 villages, grouped into 386 communes and 35 towns. Large rural areas (more than 7,000 inhabitants) are located in the plains of Diosig, Secuieni and Maramureş county. The urban system is dominated by Cluj-Napoca (330,000 inhabitants) followed by Oradea (223,000 inhabitants). On the second level there are two towns with 150,000 inhabitants (Baia Mare and Satu Mare).

The **economy** of the region is balanced, but there are some discrepancies between the six counties. The counties from the southern and western part of the region (Cluj, Bihor, and Satu Mare) are more industrialized. In these counties the manufacturing industry is more developed while in Maramureş the mining industry and metallurgy are the major industrial branches. In the Central and Eastern part of the region agriculture is dominant as well as livestock, orchards and nurseries. The tourist potential and landscape enhance the economic potential as well.

The environmental situation could be considered acceptable with a few notable exceptions. There are some polluted areas near Baia Mare and Zalău. In Baia Mare pollution is due to the mining activities and non ferrous processing activities. Air and water pollution is a problem in this area.

6.9 Conclusions

Despite the major diversity of the counties in the Northwest Region it is worth noticing the diverse cooperation possibilities due to complementary resources. The unity of this region is created by the powerful polarization of the city of Cluj-Napoca.

The privatization and restructuring of the heavy industry, and in particular the mining industry are the key problems of the region. The variety and richness of local resources ensure the future development of the industry as well as the prospects for SMEs enterprise development.

The Regional Development Agency of Northwest Region was set up in Cluj-Napoca, Cluj County. The difficulty of this location is that Cluj county is a "central" county and does not have an external frontier. However, the CBC issue is well understood in terms of strong local interests on the part of the Hungarian population of Cluj county itself. There are some well-known important Romanian-Hungarian or Hungarian Institutions, such as the Babeş-Bolyai University, the Magyar Theatre, a.s.o. In addition there is a strong interest in the region in the form of Hungarian business investments, and a good perspective for joint economic and cultural development.

Annex B

7. Institutional framework (proposal)

Objectives

To set up a cross-border structure at regional level on the Romanian side

Aims of the structure

- To provide a cross-border interface and facilitate cross-border cooperation
- To provide links and services between regional and county authorities and other private bodies and citizens
- To support long term activities in partnership

Issues to address

- The decentralization of projects management (What is the current and likely future situation with the CBC PMU ?)
- Propose a realistic design for a CBC institutional framework
- Authorization of the institutional framework
- Coordination with the Hungarian side

Preliminary remarks

1. An institutional framework that has the responsibility for the regional CBC strategy and action plan is required (this should be strongly coordinated with the regional planning frame)

2. The exchange of CBC experience will be of the benefit to a wider network of institutions with an interest in CBC

3. There are other possible areas in which such a wider CBC network could be of assistance to institutions in the region. One example is the coordination and provision of information. Another might be the search for potential partners.

4. A wider network would provide the means for all parties and institutions in regional CBC to have a platform for their opinion

5. The CBC PMU will continue its functions for the next three years but beyond that the situation remains unclear at this moment. An institutional framework therefore could begin its activities in a modest manner and still have time to adapt itself to a more extensive role in CBC in the future

Tasks

1. Identify the Romanian regional institutional framework necessary for the regional strategy and action plan

2. Identify a wider CBC network, propose and agree on a design for this as well as identify costs of setting it up and operating it

Approach

- Each county to identify possible interested institutions
- County Working Groups to consider and comment
- Coordinate responses, finalize proposal, coordinate with the Hungarian side
- Determine steps for presentation and authorization in conjunction with draft strategic priorities and objectives at regional level

Proposal for Institutional Framework to cover the Regional Strategy and Action Plan

Structure:

Three levels of decision consisting of:

1. Top decision making body for the Romanian-Hungarian CBC Region

2. Decision level for the Romanian side

3. Technical and consultative Working Group level on the Romanian side

Proposed organization:

1. The current Joint Coordinating Committee (JCC)

2. Committee consisting of the following: Presidents of the County Councils or their representatives, and Presidents of the two Regional Development Boards or their representatives

3. Permanent Working Group and secretariat consisting of: Directors of the two RDAs, 4 Directors of a coordinating institution from each county and other members coopted if necessary

Proposal for a CBC network based on a county network structure

Structure: Set up in each county a CBC coordinating office to provide a focus for the network and groups interested in CBC.

The most practical way of doing this is to set up such an office based on existing facilities. For example this might be based on:

- ADAR in Arad County
- CASTTEL in Bihor County
- CDIMM in Satu Mare County
- ADETIM in Timiş County

(Note that these offices are currently working directly in CBC with neighboring Hungarian counties and are also involved in county regional development)

An alternative is to set up a new office, but this approach is not recommended due to the uncertainty and delays that could be expected in funding.

Tasks

The tasks of this office need to be developed but an initial list could be to:

- Provide a central point in the county for all CBC issues and questions for Hungarian, regional and county public and private organisations and citizens
- Act as the county coordinating office for the continued development and implementation of the regional CBC strategy and action plan
- Coordinate CBC activities and requirements in the county
- Coordinate and facilitate information flows for members
- Provide information about CBC activities to interested persons and organizations
- Disseminate information from the CBC databases which are due to be set up in the offices of the Arad CBC regional office
- Provide PR about CBC activities and possibilities

In due course these offices could take on some of the roles of the CBC Regional office and carry out other work, including:

- Assistance in the generation of projects, the preparation of necessary fiches and training for this
- Preparing, collecting and processing project submissions
- Monitoring technical and financial progress of projects

In the same time this network could be expanded to other CBC regions in Romania.

Bibliography

ASTER TECHNICAL ASSISTANCE TEAM (1999): Regional Development Institution Building Programme (Phare, Romania), Basic Information Notes.

BUDISTEANU I. PASCARIU S. (1998): Perspectives and strategies of Spatial Development Policy in CADSES – Interreg II C – Vision Planet, Romania, National Contribution, Report.

COMMUNITY INITIATIVE INTERREG II C (1999): Vision PLANET, Policy Option Paper, Draft.

EUROPEAN COMMISSION (1999): Committee on Spatial Development, ESDP (Towards Balanced of the Territory of the EU), Potsdam.

NATIONAL COMMISSION OF STATISTICS (1998): National Statistical Yearbook - 1998.

RAMBOLL CONSULTANCY GROUPS (1997), Profiles of the Romanian Development Regions, Report.

PASCARIU S. (1998): New Communication Challenges: Local and Regional Government and EU, Paper.

PASCARIU S. (1999): Management of Phare CBC Ro/Hu Regional Study project, 1998/1999.

Contributors

MARTÍNEZ REYNÉS, MARIA ROSA, ASS.PROF.
   University of Balearic Islands, Department of Earth Sciences, Carretera de Valldemossa, km 7.5, E-07071 Palma de Mallorca - Illes Balears, Spain

ORTNER, WALTER, MAG.
   Research and Training Center for Labor and Industry (FAZAT–Steyr), Wehrgraben 1-5, A-4400 Steyr, Austria

PASCARIU, SIMONA, ARCH.
   Urbanproject Bucarest, Rue N. Filipescu 53-55, RO-70136 Bucharest 2, Romania

PERGER, WERNER A., DR.
   Die Zeit, Gerd Bucerius GmbH & Co, D-20079 Hamburg, Germany

RANTAKOKKO, MIKA
   Northern Periphery Programme Secretariat, Kauppurienkatu 8 A, FIN-90100 Oulu, Finland

SEGUÍ PONS, JOANA MARIA, PROF. DR.
   University of Balearic Islands, Department of Earth Sciences, Carretera de Valldemossa, km 7.5, E-07071 Palma de Mallorca - Illes Balears, Spain

TROEGER-WEIß, GABI, DR.
   EUREGIO EGRENSIS, Fikentscherstr. 24, D-95615 Marktredwitz, Germany

WIECHMANN, THORSTEN, DIPL.GEOGR. DR.
   Institute of Ecological and Regional Development, Division of Spatial Planning and Regional Development, Weberplatz 1, D-01217 Dresden, Germany

ZIMMERMANN, FRIEDRICH M., O.UNIV-PROF. DR.
   Institute of Geographie and Regional Science, Karl–Franzens–University of Graz, Heinrichstrasse 36, A-8010 Graz, Austria

ZONNEVELD, WILL, DR.
   Netherlands Scientific Council for Government Policy, POB 20004, NL-2500 EA Den Haag, The Netherlands